# Governance for a
# Higgledy-Piggledy Planet

# Governance for a Higgledy-Piggledy Planet

*Crafting a Balance between Local Autonomy and External Openness*

RALPH C. BRYANT

BROOKINGS INSTITUTION PRESS
*Washington, D.C.*

Copyright © 2021
THE BROOKINGS INSTITUTION
1775 Massachusetts Avenue, N.W.
Washington, D.C. 20036
www.brookings.edu

Library of Congress Control Number: 2020945852
ISBN 9780815738718 (pbk : alk. paper)
ISBN 9780815738725 (ebook)

9 8 7 6 5 4 3 2 1

Typeset in Minion Pro

# Contents

# Governance for a
# Higgledy-Piggledy Planet

# 1. Introduction

Governance compels trade-offs between independent decisions and cooperative decisionmaking. Practical choices fall between the extreme of complete decentralization for individual decisions and the opposite extreme of cooperative decisions requiring full centralization of authority. The core of governance is to identify and sustain appropriate compromise decisions for collective action.

Substantial benefits accrue to jurisdictions that are open to localities outside their borders. But external openness can also entail substantial costs. Governing institutions must weigh how much to preserve valued local autonomy while promoting desired benefits from external openness. Preservation of local separateness competes with enjoyment of benefits from unrestricted cross-border flows of people, capital, goods, ideas, technologies, and information.

Identifying compromises for managing border tensions is an inexorable headache for governance leadership. The issues arise for jurisdictions of all sizes and types. The problems are especially difficult for the two-hundred-odd nation-states that are the dominating jurisdictions in today's world polity.

The preceding sentences identify issues abstractly. Some specific examples, however, might better resonate with readers. Consider for a moment, then, instances where external openness and local autonomy are in conflict.

Suppose a local mayor were to assert that "many of our foods and medicines are imported from a foreign country where safety standards are inadequate. The foreigners even permit chlorinated washing of chicken products at the end of their production lines. Such treatments try to compensate for poor hygiene standards— for example, dirty crowded abattoirs. I do not want unsafe foods and medicines sold in my local shops. Furthermore, safety conditions for the workers on foreign production lines are less stringent than those protecting our own local workers." Some questions: Does the mayor have a convincing case for remedial actions to be taken by the foreign country? How should the foreign country react to demands for improved safety conditions? If the foreigners argue that the home case is flawed, how should the cross-border controversies be resolved?

Different border tensions arise when foreign jurisdictions are critical of the laws and regulations in a home jurisdiction. Suppose a home official charged with promoting domestic development acknowledges privately that home financial institutions are permitted to follow relatively lax regulations when lending to and accepting deposits from clients: "Our banks and legal firms do have a reputation for sailing close to the wind in monitoring cross-border money laundering. De facto, we are a tax haven for encouraging legal tax avoidance (but not evasion). Some foreign governments complain. But our country uses such regulations to promote our financial and economic growth. Moreover, we have sovereignty in these matters. It is unfair for foreign governments and international institutions to demand we adopt more stringent measures when such measures are not in our own interest."

Questions: Is this local reaction to foreign criticisms appropriate? From whose perspective? How are sovereignty and autonomy related? Should home regulators be obliged to cooperate with foreign regulators in reducing money laundering and excessive tax avoidance in the world financial system?

Local autonomy conflicts with external openness most abrasively for flows of people across borders. "*Our* homeland," complains a localist neighbor, "is inundated with foreign immigrants. Plumbers coming from Poland are taking away my indigenous clientele. Our schools are filling up with immigrant children and complicating achievement of our educational goals." A more extreme complaint is that "our cultural identity is eroding. Our homeland is filling up with foreigners. This influx *must* stop." But a group of outward-looking neighbors stresses, "Our economy needs immigrant workers to satisfy demands for seasonal agricultural labor. And on moral humanitarian grounds, we *must* provide support for asylum seekers and refugees fleeing from political persecution and natural disasters abroad." Yet other voices observe that "immigration flows result in convoluted combinations of effects on local residents. Some locals experience net gains while others suffer net losses. It is inevitable that views will differ sharply and prove politically contentious." Question: Does a practicable center of gravity exist for migration policy decisions—a sustainable middle-ground consensus—between the unrealistic extreme of unfettered freedom to cross borders and the unrealistic and inhumane exclusion of foreign migrants, including even asylum seekers and refugees?

Leave aside examples for a moment. Instead, ponder the implications of a dominant fact. The political structure of our planet is extremely complex. Its multiple jurisdictions are higgledy-piggledy: fractured, disorderly, with heads and tails in any or every direction. Why is this structure significant? The simple answer is that a higgledy-piggledy political structure can generate higgledy-piggledy governance. Decentralized decisions among noncooperating jurisdictions can, and often do, encourage damaging cross-border behaviors that undermine the mutual well-being of the jurisdictions.

This book identifies numerous instances of self-interested actions among noncooperating jurisdictions that can cause failures of mutual well-being. For individuals and small groups, such failures within jurisdictions are regularly perceived and widely understood. What is less widely perceived is how this issue permeates all aspects of cross-border interactions and how failures of international collective action are becoming gradually more detrimental. Collective-action failures that are harmful among smaller groups and jurisdictions can be especially damaging when the decentralized noncooperative decisions are made by the world's two-hundred-odd nations.

Now a metaphor: Governance in today's and tomorrow's higgledy-piggledy world is like a convoluted motorway along which diverse vehicles travel in multiple directions. The vehicles include large buses with numerous passengers, heavy and light trucks, single autos, motorcycles, even scooters and bicycles. Given the plethora of vehicles, not all drivers' decisions can be fully decentralized. Individual vehicles cannot plausibly set their own speed limits. All drivers must accept some rules of the road. Those rules need to be cooperatively agreed to among governance officials, road architects, and vehicle owners. Governing authorities must be able, when necessary, to enforce the rules.

The motorway entails the combination of individual and small-group decisions already familiar from national highways and local roads. But the planetary motorway has additional, complicated twists. It requires innovative interactive engagements. The governance units of nations are increasingly deeply involved as *decentralized* decisionmakers in a larger context. The existing planetary motorway, in effect, operates less and less smoothly without adequate rules of the road. Sadly, rules of the road and off-ramps are out of date or nonexistent. Accidents can occur more often. Greater need for improved rules and more intense cooperation requires enhanced engagement from national governments—*acting together collectively.* (As discussed in subsequent chapters, the absence of cooperation about rules of the road, and an absence of cooperation of how and where to provide off-ramps, permits greater scope for market failures (so-called "externalities") that cause more numerous and more serious accidents.)

Examples of the need for enhanced international collective action leap to mind. The classic historical illustration is the disruption in cross-border trade flows during the Great Depression. The infamous Smoot-Hawley Tariff Act in the United States (June 1930) sharply raised tariffs on thousands of categories of U.S. imports. The contention was that this decision would protect American businesses and farmers, thereby improving the U.S. economy. Many foreign nations, some in response to Smoot-Hawley, retaliated with their own enhanced restrictions on their imports. Historians and economists widely agree that the tit-for-tat escalation of import restrictions contributed to a sharp decline in international trade, harmed rather than helped the U.S. and foreign economies, and seriously exacerbated the depression. When tariffs and other trade restrictions are imposed unilaterally and aggressively, the ultimate outcome for all nations can easily become a negative-sum game in which most or all nations suffer net losses.

Conversely, history shows that cooperative international agreements will often yield a better resolution of trade policy disputes. Notably, after World War II, international sentiment for cooperative trade agreements eventually led to the creation of new international institutions such as the International Monetary Fund (IMF) in 1944, the General Agreement on Tariffs and Trade (GATT) in 1947, and ultimately the World Trade Organization (WTO) in 1994–1995.

A quintessential example for the future stems from global climate change caused by the burgeoning emissions of greenhouse gases. The climate-change crisis, as discussed in detail later, is gradually worsening. It is an existential threat for the entirety of life on the planet. Without explicit international discussions that lead to collective monitoring and enforcement mechanisms, individual nations will inevitably be entangled in a negative-sum game in which most will suffer badly. Increased collective action is essential. Cooperative multinational discussions, yielding binding international agreements, are indispensable if humanity hopes to make progress in mitigating global climate change.

Issues of financial stability in a progressively integrating world financial system are legion. For example, recall the financial panic that spread from one banking system to another in the fall of 2008 and early 2009. Without concerted cooperative intervention by the major central banks, the instabilities in financial interactions across borders could easily have been much worse and caused still sharper declines in outputs and employment. This book frequently highlights cross-border issues of instability and misbehavior in finance, and considers measures to mitigate those risks. One of the illustrative examples above already identified issues of financial cybercrime, including inappropriate encouragements of tax avoidance and money laundering.

The early years of the twenty-first century saw heightened problems resulting from the cross-border migration of people. Many international agreements about refugees and asylum seekers inherited from the twentieth century were weakened. Cooperative measures to manage the pressures for cross-border "economic" migrations (motivated by the desire to improve economic well-being) slipped backward rather than progressing forward.

Joint management of the risks from nuclear weapons have troubled national governance for decades. Tensions have not abated. Proliferation issues with additional nations have intensified. Despite episodic progress from time to time, cooperative efforts for joint monitoring and oversight of the risks have not kept adequate pace with weapons capabilities and their spread.

A catalog of governance issues with cross-border complications could be extended in numerous directions. On the optimistic, "successful" side of the catalog are examples such as the collaboration among national governments about the use of the Antarctic landmass; the Montreal Protocol of 1987, which limited the use of ozone-destroying chlorofluorocarbons; the activities of courts on several continents and of the International Court of Justice ruling on human rights violations; and efforts to mitigate the overfishing of marine life in the oceans (for example, the International Whaling Commission). On the pessimistic side, the catalog includes examples such as the absence of cross-border management of the harmful flow of misinformation through digital social media; inadequate intergovernmental guidelines for coordinating national policies for the protection (and avoidance of overprotection) of intellectual property rights; failures of cross-border collaboration to decelerate the worldwide excessive use of forests and other natural resources; and the absence, so far, of collective action among nations with space programs to reduce potential conflicts of satellite trajectories and the decentralized littering of orbital debris.

Some final introductory observations: The subject of this book, defined broadly, is the intensifying tensions confronting governance choices created by the progressive integration of our higgledy-piggledy planet. There are two practical goals. I try to clarify ideas about how to resolve the competing pulls of local autonomy and external openness. And I hope to generate new insights about the varied ways that public life, international as well as domestic, necessitates compromise combinations of decentralized decisions and cooperative interactions.

My life as an economist has focused on interdependent nations. This book follows naturally from that earlier work. But my aspirations here differ somewhat. I step back from particulars and instead highlight fundamentals. My strategy is to analyze governance choices viewed broadly for the planet as a whole. Hence I focus on the major parts of the landscape's topography. I suppress many details, instead surveying the landscape as if seen by an eagle flying high overhead.

Some readers might feel ill at ease with this eagle's-flight perspective. An overview cannot avoid focusing on analytic fundamentals. But that requirement does create difficulties. Several colleagues have advised me to de-emphasize my analytical focus. They fear that some readers may become impatient with abstract framing of issues. They correctly point out that many people are less interested in the basic issues of collective governance than in analyzing specific examples.

These difficulties have shaped my writing. Yet I have stubbornly resisted the idea of deleting analytical basics. Only when fundamentals are lucid is it possible to achieve clarity about specific details. Reliable insights require an integrated perspective of the entire landscape.

An overview necessitates some trespassing on the turf of other social science disciplines. One cannot obtain an eagle's perspective without venturing well outside narrowly defined economics, and the potential net gains justify any perceived trespassing. (When economics is understood expansively, there is no trespassing.) If this overview should misrepresent facts or truths, future updates from the other disciplines will identify needed revisions.

My generalizations here are targeted at diverse participants on the metaphorical motorway. I most hope to reach policymakers and leaders directly responsible for these issues—those who design and revise the rules of the road, those who drive the largest buses, those enforcers who try to keep vehicles from going astray. Simultaneously, I hope to reach many bus and car passengers who are just engaged participants.

The analysis here makes a strong normative plea for enhanced international cooperation in governance choices. Such cooperation will become more essential in the turbulent future that lies ahead. The tone of my writing tilts toward pessimism, on occasion perhaps even unduly. This tilt is easily explained. In recent years the largest political jurisdictions in the world took unwise, adverse turns on the motorway. Sadly, thoughtful cross-border collective action frequently slipped backward. My own nation, the United States, was a major contributor to the backsliding, undermining its previous global leadership and foolishly creating dangerous doubts about future American credibility. This recent experience has led me to focus on issues where collective governance across jurisdictional borders has been inadequate.

I do not believe, nor want to imply, that progress in international cooperation has been inconsequential. On the contrary, throughout history and in numerous substantive areas, examples of cross-border cooperation have been prominent and unambiguously favorable. Analyses by scholars of international relations have produced a sizable literature.

When struggling with these issues, one needs to maintain perspective, to achieve a balance between pessimism and optimism. Nurturing international comity and enhancing cooperation are essential for a safe, sustainable evolution of the planet and its multiple jurisdictions. The world community must somehow gradually construct future rules of the road that are stronger, mutually beneficial, and better maintained. Every public-minded person should be concerned about improving collective governance for the individual jurisdictions and the planet where their children and grandchildren hope to prosper.

No Man is an *Iland*, intire of it selfe;
every man is a peece of the *Continent*, a part of the *maine*;
if a Clod be washed away be the *Sea*, *Europe* is the lesse,
as well as if a *Promontorie* were,
as well as if a *Mannor* of thy *friends*, or of *thine owne* were ....
Any Mans *death* diminishes *me*, because I am involved in *Mankinde*;
therefore never send to know for whom the *bell* tolls;
It tolls for *thee*.

*John Donne*, Devotions upon Emergent Occasions, *Meditation 17*

# 2. Analytic Fundamentals

*Jurisdiction* is a generic term for polity or society. *Jurisdiction* and *subjurisdiction* are words not widely used in ordinary discourse. *Identity space, decision space, governing authority, externality,* and *market failure* are other less familiar terms. Discussion of borders and trade-offs permeates this book. These terms and the ideas underpinning them are analytic building blocks for what follows. Clarity necessitates identifying them at the outset.

## Identity Spaces, Decision Spaces, Jurisdictions, Governing Authorities

An individual's views of who he or she is, and wants to be, shape a life in profound ways. Insights about identity apply not only to individuals but also to identities shared among groups. Identity spaces are defined by "belonging" with others who share similar identities. Social norms are grounded in shared perceptions of social identities.[1]

Decision spaces are arrangements through which collective decisions are made. Governance decisions for jurisdictions are catalyzed and implemented by governing institutions—the "governance units" or "governing authorities"—for those jurisdictions.

Many smaller jurisdictions are identity spaces and decision spaces that link participants in ethnic, religious, or cultural organizations. Larger jurisdictions range from counties, municipalities, and provinces up a vertical dimension to still higher levels of nation-states and even international institutions.

The dominating facts about the planet's jurisdictions are their higgledy-piggledy differences—differences in sizes and resources; differences in the ethnic, racial, and religious characteristics of their residents; differences in their social, cultural, and political histories; and differences in types of governing authorities. Smaller jurisdictions may or may not have territorial boundaries. Many jurisdictions are horizontally separate geographical spaces. Larger jurisdictions, especially those with multiple vertical layers, do typically have geographical borders. Jurisdictions with vertical layers of governance contain nested subjurisdictions.

Because of jurisdictional heterogeneity, generalizations about governance choices and policy responses are themselves higgledy-piggledy and therefore fraught with difficulties. The complexities are especially severe for multilayer jurisdictions that practice some variety of federalist governance. Lower-level political layers

---

1. Akerlof and Kranton, *Identity Economics: How Our Identities Shape Our Work, Wages, and Well-Being* (2011). See also, for example, Helliwell (2015, 2000); Helliwell et al. (2014); Maier (2016); Putnam (2000a, 2000b); Egginton (2018).

have significant local autonomy but are overseen by upper-level governing authorities.[2]

The residents of larger geographical jurisdictions pursue multitudinous goals. They practice varying cultures and traditions. They espouse multiple identities. Sometimes the goals, cultures, and identities are shared. Often they are different and competing, even within—and especially across—jurisdictions. Pronounced contrasts exist in internal heterogeneity, in social cohesion, and in capacities to attain consensus decisions.

Successful jurisdictions nonetheless make collective decisions. Governance authorities have powers to influence social identities and norms. Their policy actions are anvils on which collective decisions are designed and stamped. Governance arrangements are thus continually under stress, subject to criticism from residents and from outsiders.

*Governance* should not be used as a synonym for *government.* Actions taken by or through government institutions are the primary forms of collective governance. But governance encompasses collective action channeled not only through public-sector government but also through nongovernment activities that are not part of government at any level. Governance is the more comprehensive of the concepts. It subsumes the entirety of institutions and relationships involved in governance activities. The broad concept of governance and the narrower concept of government both entail purposeful collaborative behavior underpinned by a presumptive sharing of goals.[3]

2. For example, the United States, China, India, France, Nigeria, and notably the European Union. The specific allocations of governance responsibilities between the upper level and the various lower levels vary greatly across jurisdictions, and especially across those with multiple layers.

3. Public-sector government is typically backed by formal authority, legal powers to ensure implementation and compliance with collectively decided policies. For other governance, the shared goals may not derive from legal and

For the individuals and groups affected, decentralized decisions can produce inferior outcomes. Cooperation among decisionmakers—actions taken collectively rather than independently without cooperation—can produce superior outcomes. That is because, again, the core of governance is to identify and sustain appropriate compromise decisions for collective action.

## Externalities, Market Failures, Public Goods, Governance Failures

Analysts use the labels *externalities* and *market failures* to describe inferior outcomes that can result from decentralized, uncoordinated decisions. Externalities cause market failures. Provision of *public goods* can rectify market failures.

An externality is said to occur when an activity by one agent affects the well-being of other agents who are not decisionmaking participants in that activity. Externalities cause economic inefficiencies because the costs (benefits) to individual agents differ from the costs (benefits) for society as a whole.[4]

---

formally prescribed responsibilities. Private-sector groups may have only weak powers to ensure compliance. Another difference between governance and government stems from the comprehensiveness of the jurisdictions through which collective action is fostered. Because the broad notion embraces the activities of smaller, narrowly limited jurisdictions as well as larger, widely inclusive jurisdictions, governance subsumes all of "civil society," loosely defined as the numerous groups and associations that are neither commercial nor governmental. A government institution typically derives its legal authority from the entirety of individuals in the territorial jurisdiction where the governmental collective action is exercised.

4. Polluting smoke from a factory that causes discomfort to neighborhood residents creates a negative externality. A favorable externality occurs when a homeowner beautifies the landscaping on his or her lot, thereby raising property values and improving the attractiveness of living in the neighborhood for other residents. More precise definitions of externalities require that the utility

Remedial actions collectively try, as social scientists say, to "internalize the externalities." Remedial actions might take the form of drafting of laws and regulations, and of establishing mechanisms for monitoring and administration by governance institutions. More generally, to use the language of social scientists, collective actions attempt to supply public goods or ameliorate public bads. In the absence of cooperative remedial action, public goods are provided inadequately, if provided at all; similarly, public bads are inadequately ameliorated. Public goods have one or both of two distinctive properties: If a public good is provided, all who value it tend to benefit whether or not they contribute to the cost of providing it. And if a public good is provided to anyone, it can often be provided at little or no additional cost to others.[5]

A market failure occurs if decentralized independent decisions fail to result in efficient allocation of scarce resources. Externalities of some sort are typically the cause of market failures. Externalities might not cause a significant misallocation of resources if transaction costs are negligible and if property rights are well defined and enforceable. In many practical situations, however, property rights are not or cannot be well defined. Transaction costs are often non-negligible. Thus there will exist, in particular circumstances, a potential role for some form of centralization of decisions to try to correct market failures through collective governance.

---

or production relationships for, say, agents B and C be affected by variables chosen by agent A when A does not pay attention to the effects on the welfares of B and C. If A were to receive or pay compensation for the activity that gives rise to costs or benefits for B and C, the situation would not qualify as an externality that creates inefficiency and resource misallocation. The technical economics literature also makes other distinctions, such as that between pecuniary versus technological externalities.

5. Social scientists label these two distinctive properties nonexcludability and nonrivalry in consumption.

The design and implementation of public goods pose special difficulties. All who value a public good benefit when it is supplied, whether or not they contribute to the cost of supplying it. Therefore if a public good is supplied at all, a disproportionate share of the cost tends to be borne by a few "less small" participants in the collective decision. "Free riders," so labeled because they enjoy benefits without contributing to costs, inhibit cooperative decisionmaking and reduce the supply of the public good below the levels that would be mutually beneficial. The larger the number of decisionmaking entities involved, the higher the probability that some of them will act as free riders and, hence, the less likely that all entities together will further their mutual interests.[6, 7]

The existence of market failures and the propensity for free-riding behavior is not a compelling reason for concluding that a jurisdiction should dispense with markets and decentralized decisionmaking. Collective governance can itself be costly or misguided, resulting in a *governance failure*. Even collective actions organized through smaller, nongovernment groups can be ill-advised and counterproductive.[8] Interventions by government

6. Mancur Olson, *The Logic of Collective Action: Public Goods and the Theory of Groups* (1965, 1971).

7. George Akerlof and Robert Shiller have recently emphasized yet another reason why markets with exclusively decentralized decisions may produce market failures. "When there are completely free markets, there is not only freedom to choose; there is also freedom to phish." For Akerlof-Shiller, "phishermen" are individuals seeking to manipulate others, to persuade targeted others ("phools") to do things in the interest of the phishermen but not in the true interest of the targeted phools. George A. Akerlof and Robert J. Shiller, *Phishing for Phools: The Economics of Manipulation & Deception* (2015, pp. 1–11, 149–62).

8. Not all unfortunate instances of collective action deserve to be labeled governance failures. When some participants in private nongovernmental transactions act as "phishermen" seeking to manipulate or deceive other participants as

institutions might have still higher probabilities of going awry. Government bureaucracies, like large private organizations, can sometimes be rigid, heavy-handed, and inefficient in implementing their objectives. Bureaucracies can be captured by special interests or even undermined by explicit corruption, thereby creating negative externalities themselves.[9]

It is a basic characteristic of market capitalism that market extremes and decentralized decisions can lead to market failures. It is a basic characteristic of politics that governance extremes and rigidities can lead to governance failures. Virtually every jurisdiction therefore has some combination of decentralized markets and government infrastructures.

Most larger jurisdictions throughout the world are characterized by "mixed" decisionmaking. Especially for economic matters, jurisdictions rely heavily on decentralized decisions coordinated through price signals in markets. Markets generate consistency among the decentralized decisions. The economic needs of individuals and smaller groups are heterogeneous and complex. Decentralized decisionmaking expressed through markets is often the least inefficient way for a jurisdiction to cope with this diversity and complexity. At the same time, jurisdictions acknowledge valid reasons for avoiding exclusive reliance on markets. Collective governance fosters cooperation when

"phools," the transactions are collective actions embodying voluntary behavior. But the collective actions are *private-sector* failures harmful to the genuine interests of the phools. Akerlof and Shiller (2015, pp. 1–11, 149–162).

9. To state the obvious, some public-goods actions and policy initiatives taken by a jurisdiction's governing authorities may not even be wise and commendable on their own terms, let alone be condemned as governance failures because they fail while attempting to rectify externalities and market failures. Chapter 7 will discuss the possible use by national governments of tariffs as hostile policy instruments when trying to achieve a home nation's goals at the expense of the well-being of residents of foreign nations.

decentralized decisionmaking emerging from markets would otherwise cause inferior outcomes.

The mixed capitalist economic systems of most jurisdictions therefore emphasize decentralized decisionmaking in markets but also accord major roles to governance interventions. Even the strongest proponents of free enterprise and decentralized market decisions recognize the need for an appropriate framework of laws and regulations, and for practical definitions of private property rights.[10]

## Trade-offs

A trade-off is a compromise between two incompatible goals. When goals are incompatible, neither can be fully achieved without sacrificing at least some part of the other.

Full local autonomy (autarky) and unfettered external openness, for example, cannot both be attained simultaneously. More local autonomy typically entails some surrender of the benefits of openness. Greater external openness typically entails foregoing some benefits of local autonomy. The two have to be balanced against each other.

The presence of a trade-off does not mean that everything that is good for one goal is always bad for the other. For example, some policies and behaviors that reduce local autonomy, like a cooperative agreement with other nations that produces valuable home benefits, are desirable even though they augment external openness. Some policies or behaviors that diminish exter-

---

10. Art Okun stressed this basic insight more than four decades ago: "the functioning—indeed, the very life—of the market depends on the coercive powers of political institutions." Arthur M. Okun, *Equality and Efficiency: The Big Tradeoff* (Brookings Institution, 1975; 2015, p. 31). The insight has been time and time again acknowledged even by ardent advocates of decentralized independent decisions.

nal openness, such as using a border buffer to limit access to the home financial system by foreign criminals, beneficially augment local autonomy without undermining basic policy objectives associated with external openness.

Nonetheless, the two polar goals of a trade-off typically do conflict. When discussing many such conflicts and the problems they pose, the dominant theme is the trade-off—for individual jurisdictions and the entire planet—between local autonomy and external openness.

The trade-off between local autonomy and external openness, and the still more fundamental trade-off between decentralized independent decisions and centralized cooperative decisions, exists at the core of all levels of governance. The compromises that best promote the goals of jurisdictions are sites of consensus located in the middle of a spectrum between the endpoint extremes. To be sustainable, the compromises must be politically feasible and generate reasonably wide support. At best, the compromises will be uneasy. A chosen consensus is, in effect, a center of gravity along the spectrum.

## Benefits of External Openness

If a jurisdiction's residents could not trade with residents of other jurisdictions ("foreigners"), the pattern of residents' spending would have to slavishly match the goods produced at home. So long as *relative prices* differ at home and outside, however, residents can unambiguously improve their consumption and investment possibilities by exchanging goods with foreigners. Such *exchange gains* can be augmented by *production gains*. Production gains result when the structure of production in a jurisdiction becomes specialized along the lines of *comparative advantage*. Resource and factor endowments are used more efficiently when production is specialized, permitting the jurisdiction to sell domestic production at favorable relative prices to outsiders, which in turn raises residents' consumption and investment possibilities still further.

Local residents cannot conduct cross-border transactions in goods and services, and reap the associated benefits, without permitting a commensurate degree of openness for financial transactions. Goods and services can be straightforwardly exchanged with foreigners only if the corresponding financial payments and receipts can be readily consummated. For efficiency, lending and borrowing associated with goods transactions and their settlement are also required. Changes in cross-border assets and liabilities are a necessary counterpart of goods and services transactions.

Summaries of the economic benefits of cross-border transactions usually focus on trade in goods and services. Properly construed, the fundamental points identifying the benefits from openness and comparative advantage apply to all types of cross-border transactions. For example, some jurisdictions tend to have a comparative advantage in the provision of financial services. As with goods, trade in financial services yields exchange gains and production gains. The same reasoning applies to exchanges of ideas and knowledge, even to social and cultural exchanges. Benefits associated with cross-border transactions accrue to both the "importing" and the "exporting" jurisdictions.

Potential net benefits can accrue when a local jurisdiction has access to "foreign" savings. Borrowing savings from outside can help when the jurisdiction has unexploited investment opportunities. Economic activity and well-being fall short of their potential levels if local investments must be restricted to the savings that the local economy itself is currently generating. Without flows of savings across borders, the time profile of the aggregate consumption plus investment of residents would have to conform precisely to the time profile of aggregate domestic production. Similarly, residents' aggregate savings would have to be exactly equal to their aggregate investment.

When cross-border financial intermediation severs the otherwise rigid link between savings and investment for a jurisdiction, the resulting gains are analogous to the benefits that domestic financial intermediation brings to individual households and firms. The intertemporal pattern of households' aggregate spending over time can be matched to their needs and preferences instead of having to conform with the intertemporal pattern of their earnings. Just as individual firms can hedge against events that could alter the profitability of their operations, an entire jurisdiction can collectively hedge against the future by accumulating income-earning assets held outside the jurisdiction. Just as adventurous individual producers willing to assume the basic risks of business enterprise can borrow funds in excess of their current cash flow, a jurisdiction with better than average investment prospects can assume greater than average risks by importing capital funds and real resources from outside, thereby raising future consumption possibilities for the jurisdiction.

With individual jurisdictions able to alter the intertemporal profiles of their consumption, the entire world—each city, province, nation—can attain an improved allocation of savings and investment. Jurisdictions with ex ante excess savings can employ them in jurisdictions where the ex ante return to investment is higher. Financial prices and valuations within jurisdictions respond promptly and sensitively to new information. The cross-border transactions that increasingly link jurisdictions together respond at least as rapidly and sensitively.[11]

The favorable aspects of these information signals are significant. The prompt transmittal of information within and among jurisdictions helps to generate the exchange and production

---

11. Market transactions in the aggregate, though highly sensitive, are not reliably accurate. Market decisionmakers, even for large groups, can misperceive underlying realities.

gains from cross-border transactions. Similarly, cross-border capital flows facilitate the transfer of knowledge and expertise, particularly when some or all of the capital flows are direct investments. Such benefits would not be realized to the same extent in a world in which information was disseminated less fully and less promptly. The transmission of information among geographically separated jurisdictions has accelerated enormously in recent decades. The information benefits from cross-border financial intermediation have increased correspondingly.

The fundamental point for a nation as a whole is that capital flowing across its borders allows a nation's residents to enjoy higher standards of living than would otherwise be possible—time paths of consumption that are higher, better adapted to national preferences, and not rigidly tied to the peculiarities of their geography. National investment decisions do not have to be inflexibly linked to national saving decisions. Financial prices and valuations within a nation's financial system respond promptly to new information, which further enhances economic efficiency.[12]

Yes, caution is called for when borrowing from outside. It constrains a jurisdiction and might entail a loss of local control. Yes, the sensitivity of local financial activity to cross-border transactions can be a major source of difficulty. Abrupt reversals of inflows of foreign savings can be disruptive (discussed further below). Yet the jurisdiction can on balance be better off with the borrowed savings and some reduction in its autonomy than it would be without the borrowed savings.

Freedom for financial transactions across borders permits residents to hold their assets as they wish, not only inside but also outside the nation. If one holds the normative views that individuals should be free to receive information from anywhere in

---

12. For more detailed discussion, see Bryant, *Turbulent Waters: Cross-Border Finance and International Governance* (2003).

the world, to express their views openly, to travel freely not only at home but abroad, and to buy and sell both home-produced and foreign-produced goods and services, the freedom to invest one's wealth anywhere in the world is a logical concomitant to the other freedoms.

Relatively unfettered cross-border financial transactions exert discipline on a nation's governing authorities. The unfettered capital flows help to hold a nation politically accountable. The ability of foreigners and home residents to pull funds out of the financial system forces the nation to behave better—for example, to refrain from unsustainable economic policies—than it might otherwise behave. When the nation pursues policies perceived as exemplary, furthermore, that behavior might induce net capital inflows, thereby enhancing national well-being. In effect, participants in world financial markets vote continuously with their wallets in an ongoing election about the soundness of national policies.

A further practical point: The governing authorities of a nation can erect nonporous barriers to cross-border financial transactions only with difficulty. Administrative costs might be sizable. Such barriers would to some degree cause resource misallocations in the wider economy. Pressures would be severe to make administrative exceptions. Such exceptions in turn would enhance opportunities for governance failures—notably, capture by special interests or even outright corruption.

## Costs and Risks of External Openness

The costs and risks of external openness likewise demand careful scrutiny. Individual firms and workers of a nation can lose their jobs and incomes because of disruptive shifts in trade—if, for example, goods and services produced locally are displaced by increases in competitively priced imports. Borrowing from or lending to other nations can be excessive, just as individual firms or individual households can imprudently borrow too much. Mishaps and instability in cross-border finance are all too possible. Moreover, even when a jurisdiction's own policies are sound, the jurisdiction's financial system can be whipsawed by turbulence originating externally from the behavior of outside investors. Openness to the outside world leads inevitably to vulnerability.

The concepts of sticky capital, skittish capital, voice, and exit can be helpful in discussing financial vulnerability.

Some creditors perceive their initial investing commitments as temporarily nonreversible. This is most true for investors focusing on the longer run. Investments with a longer time horizon often exhibit properties of what has been labeled *sticky capital*. Such investments are contingent at the outset on whether the fortunes of the borrower will evolve satisfactorily in conformity with the initial long-run commitment. Of course, commitments envisaging profits and returns over a longer run, such as commonly associated with foreign direct investment (FDI) across borders, are not inflexible. Commitments, especially long-run, are highly sensitive to the legal and market environment in which the investment is undertaken. The degree of stickiness for any given investment thus can change, even on short notice.

Numerous investors and creditors, however, may be preoccupied only with their expected returns over a short-run horizon. Their investments can turn volatile. With perhaps merely minor alterations in information or expectations, such commitments can suddenly switch from transitorily certain to quixotically footloose. Such investors can be little concerned with borrowers' long-run profitability and stability. Unrestricted extensions of credit with a time horizon limited to the short run—or, similarly, footloose market purchases of equity shares—exhibit properties associated with what can be termed *skittish capital*.

Differences are not clear-cut between investments behaving as sticky and those with a propensity for skittish behavior. Investments have multiple traits. Those traits can change over time. The sticky and skittish labels are best used to refer to the two outer ranges of a spectrum with many intermediate and changing points. The sticky-skittish spectrum in turn correlates with the spectrum running from voice to exit.

Choices between voice and exit in political and economic life were originally analyzed by Albert Hirschman.[13] From the perspective of an individual lender, the possibility of selling or otherwise terminating a credit to a borrower, thus transferring his or her wealth to a different asset, is an option of *exit*. Rather than remaining engaged in the activities of a borrower trying to favorably influence the behavior of the borrower, a skittish capitalist may choose to withdraw his or her wealth altogether. Such disengagement entails walking away—in effect, out an easy exit—rather than loyally staying involved to try to exert a constructive influence. When capital investments over the shorter run manifest substantial stickiness, they exert the option of *voice*, remaining loyal at least for a while. Investors whose behavior is dominated by a skittish preoccupation for only the short run have little compunction about heading for the exit on slight provocation.[14]

13. Albert O. Hirschman, *Exit, Voice, and Loyalty: Responses to Decline in Firms, Organizations, and States* (1970).

14. Several early readers of this book strongly endorsed the distinctions between voice and exit, and between sticky and skittish capital. One early reader was more wary, emphasizing (correctly) that the top priority of capital investment owners is to retain their ownership. Foreign direct investments in a home nation have a larger voice about local regulations and customs (for better or for ill). But even foreign direct investments can also turn volatile quickly and try to relocate to other jurisdictions. A recipient nation with unsound domestic policies and weak property rights can greatly undermine its ability to attract stable capital inflows and can discourage foreign owners of capital from wanting to exercise voice rather than exit. Wise home policymakers should avoid an emphasis on "wrong" behavior of capital owners and instead emphasize adoption of sound policies that encourage stable investments for both the longer and shorter runs.

Financial problems for a nation's governing authorities can easily become a conundrum. To an uncertain degree, and frequently in undesired directions, externally generated forces can enhance external vulnerability. The external forces threaten the attainment of domestic economic and social targets. Increases in financial openness diminish the influence that home governing authorities can exert over national target variables. Policy decisions become more difficult to make and more uncertain in their consequences. It becomes more difficult to maintain financial conditions at home that diverge greatly from financial conditions elsewhere in the world. The enhanced risks include informational asymmetries, adverse selection, and moral-hazard issues that are exacerbated by cross-border capital flow. Potential fragilities are compounded by herding behavior and contagion in financial markets. Asset prices may temporarily become excessively volatile. The prompt and sensitive responses of financial markets to new information can be a blessing. But this sensitivity is a double-edged sword, enhancing the risks of instability.

Risks of financial instability for the home nation are aggravated by the exit options available to domestic residents and to foreign creditors. Those exit options limit home policy choices because they give individuals, firms, and financial institutions the freedom to transfer assets out of the nation. This freedom can at times be a constructive discipline on governmental decisions. But, again, the benefits of shifting assets and liabilities freely out of or into the nation is a double-edged sword, generating added risks for the nation as a whole, even as it enhances the freedom of individual economic agents.

Foreign investors, enthusiastic this month about future prospects for the home nation's economy and unconcerned about current government policies, may ladle funds into the domestic financial system with abandon. But next month or next year—perhaps with a valid trigger for their actions, but perhaps not—

fickle foreign investors might rush for the exits and cause severe disruption to the home economy's evolution. Unfettered capital flows can exert constructive discipline but then act in whipsaw fashion to destabilize the nation's financial system and economy.[15]

A person attracted to completely unfettered capital flows should consider a remark made by the minister of finance from a relatively small developing nation. Large capital flows surging into his nation, the minister observed, reminded him of elephants trampling in a pond, making it muddy. He acknowledged that capital flows surging into a large nation might be analogous to elephants moving into the forest, where they may get lost in the general environment and cause little commotion. But if your nation is more like a smaller pond, he warned, watch out!

Investments with a longer time horizon in the home economy where the capital initially has stickiness are, other things being equal, preferable to investments easily associated with skittish behavior. Sticky capital is somewhat more likely to exercise voice in stormy weather. Capital easily accompanied by skittish behavior may precipitously use the exit option. Inward direct investment from abroad, therefore, is usually more stable and more beneficial than bank loans from abroad or from foreigners' lending in other short-term forms. Yet financial activity without potentially skittish capital is impossible, either within nations or across national borders. All capital is eventually skittish to some extent. The best a nation can do is to encourage policies that nurture the stickiness of capital (especially inward foreign direct investment) and that establish prudent guidelines for avoiding excessive exposures to the most skittish forms of foreign capital. Policies to

---

15. Transactions in financial futures markets and the proliferation of complex derivative transactions have further increased the volatility of cross-border capital flows and exchange-rate movements.

encourage the stickiness of capital cannot alone assure financial stability.

## Distribution of the Net Benefits and
## Net Costs of External Openness

The preceding observations stress the benefits and risks of external openness without specifying which resident entities are most likely to reap large benefits or experience significant adversity. Most expositions describing the analytic fundamentals use nation-states as exemplar jurisdictions. This book likewise will increasingly focus on nation-states. But the reasoning about comparative advantage and the benefits of external openness applies to jurisdictions and subjurisdictions of all types, not merely to nations in the global economy.

Who among individual insiders bears the potential costs of external openness? Which residents enjoy benefits? When speaking about any jurisdiction or aggregation of jurisdictions, it is essential to distinguish between gross benefits and net benefits.

From a planetary perspective, gross benefits stemming from external openness—potential and actual—are probably huge. Empirical evidence to support that planetary generalization is not readily available. But theory and the historical experiences of multiple individual jurisdictions point in that direction. Again, residents of externally open jurisdictions can enjoy higher standards of living—time paths of consumption that are higher, better adapted to their particular preferences, and not rigidly tied to the peculiarities of their geographical circumstances. What is true for individual subjurisdictions such as provinces or municipalities is true for individual nation-states. Indeed, the principle of comparative advantage has bedrock validity for the planet as a whole. Cross-border transactions among externally open jurisdictions increase worldwide consumption possibilities because they permit a more efficient allocation of world resources than could otherwise occur. Noneconomic benefits may be even more salient.

For individual jurisdictions and specific residents, however, one must appraise costs and therefore analyze benefits that are net as well as gross. Gross costs can be large for particular residents. Net benefits for them may be sizably negative. For an entire jurisdiction, those costs can be a highly significant offset to the net benefits enjoyed by other residents. For the jurisdiction as a whole, net benefits may well be unambiguously positive. But it would be a humanitarian and political mistake to underestimate or ignore the net costs experienced by particular residents.

For nations, aggregate net benefits can vary significantly across time. Net benefits can vary for citizens versus noncitizen residents. Typically, net gains are proportionately larger for smaller nations and for nations with relatively poor endowments of natural resources. Hence such nations could be severely disadvantaged if they choose to forego many of the benefits from external openness.

The net gains from some types of cross-border transactions are much more consequential than the net gains from other types. For many locals, progressively easier access to foreign educational, social, and cultural resources may seem more valuable than ever before. The benefits from innovations in communications and transportation technologies that continue to shrink the effective distances among jurisdictions are especially important (though the costs are substantial, too).

What about citizen and noncitizen residents who suffer net losses instead of reaping net benefits? More broadly, how are the losses and gains from external openness distributed among residents of a jurisdiction?

The unfortunate awkward truth is that particular individuals or particular factors of production can be badly harmed by external openness. The harm can be permanent rather than merely temporary. Sectors of a jurisdiction's economy specializing in particular goods that become obsolete because of changes in consumer preferences, technological innovations, or competitively priced imports suffer losses as resources are allocated away from those sectors.

The incidence of harmful economic effects is greatest in local labor or product markets in which the activities exposed to outside competition are concentrated. The outside competition necessitates adjustment costs that fall disproportionately on those local citizens. Distributional consequences can be so severe that exposed firms and workers may experience reduced lifetime incomes.

Increasing integration has heightened the possibilities for adverse distributional consequences. Nation-states, not least the more advanced developed nations, have progressively experienced the distribution tensions. On average, dislocations and gross costs for particular individuals and groups may well have become proportionately more salient through time.

Business and financial interests are the driving forces promoting cross-border transactions. Those interests are typically better placed—offer easier political access and greater political powers—to influence national policies affecting such transactions. Individuals whose interests are partly in conflict with business and financial interests may believe, often justifiably, that their well-being is insufficiently protected in governance decisions. Not surprisingly, assertions about unfair distributional consequences of external openness frequently surface in national political discourse.

Because the distributional consequences of external openness can be so striking, collective governance could and should helpfully respond. When the gross benefits to beneficiaries exceed the losses experienced by those adversely affected, which is typically the case, opportunities exist at least in principle for collective-action adjustments. Gainers can help losers by sharing some of their gains. The compensation to losers requires redistributing only a portion of the gross gains; beneficiaries of the large gross benefits can still be left with substantially positive post-redistributive outcomes.

Potential redistributive adjustments could include programs for retraining workers who lose jobs, educational opportunities for learning new skills, incentives for the establishment of new types of production facilities, and expenditures for research and development. Such programs should ideally be focused on the local areas most affected by the competitive disruptions.[16] Although employment protection legislation can reduce displacement of workers and industries, it can also impede needed reallocation of workers to newly profitable activities.[17] Perhaps most important, adversely affected resident citizens can receive direct subsidies or compensation payments.[18]

16. See, for example, Jay Shambaugh and Ryan Nunn, eds., *Place-Based Policies for Shared Economic Growth*, Washington DC (Brookings Institution, Hamilton Project, 2018); and Benjamin Austin, Edward Glaeser, and Lawrence Summers, "Saving the Heartland: Place-Based Policies in 21st Century America," *Brookings Papers on Economic Activity* (Spring 2018). For an overview of "left-behind" areas in the United States and the need to better adapt redistributive policies to those spaces, see Clara Hendrickson, Mark Muro, and William A. Galston, "Countering the Geography of Discontent: Strategies for Left-Behind Places" (2018).

17. A joint IMF-World Bank-WTO paper submitted to the G20 in 2017 reported, "There is broad consensus that employment protection should be limited, and [instead] that low hiring/firing costs coupled with protection through unemployment benefits is preferable. . . . Similarly, minimum wage policies can protect low-skilled workers from exploitation and ensure that they earn a basic level of income; however, the policies need to be designed carefully to avoid potentially negative employment and efficiency effects; an overly high minimum wage, coupled with high payroll taxes, can hinder employment prospects of vulnerable groups. . . . Well-designed and targeted trade-specific support programs can complement existing labor-market programs." *Making Trade an Engine of Growth for All: The Case for Trade and for Policies to Facilitate Adjustment.* Paper available on International Monetary Fund website.

18. "Some type of income transfer, such as means-tested support or early retirement for older workers, is often provided to displaced workers who no

Sadly, in practice it is extraordinarily difficult to implement remedial collective actions to achieve the compensating redistribution of gross benefits. The associated problems are among the most complex of all political issues inhibiting the consensuses required for compromise trade-offs. Politicians and pundits have found it much easier to pay lip service to the need for compensating redistribution than to mobilize support for actually implementing it. The familiar reluctance for centralized cooperation often inhibits outcomes that would otherwise be mutually beneficial for a large majority of residents.

## Tensions between Local Autonomy and External Openness

Tensions between the competing goals of local autonomy and external openness are, again, rooted in the elemental trade-off between decentralized independent decisions and cooperative centralized decisionmaking. Local autonomy emphasizes separateness. Localist decisions may give little or no weight to outsiders. External openness undermines the ability to sustain local conditions that desirably differ from cultural, economic, and social conditions elsewhere. Yet efforts to shield a jurisdiction from unwanted foreign influences may simultaneously require the sacrifice of significant cultural, economic, and social gains—hence reducing improvements in well-being. The pervasive forces

---

longer qualify for unemployment insurance. In countries where disability insurance screening is not particularly stringent, these transfers can de-facto become an important form of long-term income support. Meanwhile, health insurance can also be part of the policy design, especially in countries where access to affordable health services is more limited. More generally, reliance on these other social insurance and income support programs is often costly and efforts should be made to minimize incidences of dislocated workers dropping out of the labor force." International Monetary Fund, World Bank, and World Trade Organization (2017).

of increasing cross-border spillover further intensify the difficulties in finding balanced decisions about the competing goals.

The smaller and more open a polity and its economy, the steeper the trade-off is likely to be. Toward the extremes of smallness and openness, the ability through local policies to nurture indigenous culture, institutions, and identifiably separate local conditions may be so limited as to seem negligible. When jurisdictional polities and economies are large and less open, the trade-off may still be relatively steep. Yet at least the tensions are less than with extreme openness.

Some commentators have argued that for practical purposes, the trade-off between autonomy and openness does not exist, even for large polities and economies. Writing about the choices facing an individual nation, for example, Thomas Friedman asserted the inevitability of a "Golden Straitjacket," an ideology recommending few constraints on free-market capitalism.[19] But a recommendation for market fundamentalism for all nations, or even for national subjurisdictions, is an extreme position. That hyperglobalization extreme gives exclusive primacy to economic efficiency (not always reliably achieved) and overlooks the possibilities of a middle ground.

---

19. "The historical debate is over. The answer is free-market capitalism [in a global economy]. . . . Ideologically, there is no more mint chocolate chip, there is no more strawberry swirl, and there is no more lemon-lime. Today there is only free-market vanilla and North Korea. . . . In the end, if you want higher standards of living in a world without walls, the free market is the only ideological alternative left. One road. Different speeds. But one road. When [a] country recognizes this fact, when it recognizes the rules of the free market in today's global economy, and decides to abide by them, it puts on what I call 'the Golden Straitjacket.' The Golden Straitjacket is the defining political-economic garment of this globalization era. The Cold War had the Mao suit, the Nehru jacket, the Russian fur. Globalization has only the Golden Straitjacket. If your country has not been fitted for one, it will be soon." Thomas Friedman, *The Lexus and the Olive Tree* (1999, p. 86).

A jurisdiction's residents—justifiably, albeit sometimes excessively—value the preservation of indigenous norms and institutions, and the retention of local decisionmaking. Hence residents give significant priority to local attitudes and local goals. The tendency to favor localism—selfishly to advance "our own" interests relative to those of "foreigners"—can be especially powerful if homogeneity within the jurisdiction is strong and if jurisdictional loyalty and cohesion are deeply rooted. The extreme version of centripetal localism is to yearn for a "great wall" that insulates home residents from unwanted influences originating in the outside world.

Governance choices for individual jurisdictions—most notably, nations—might appear simple if policymakers could straightforwardly sign up for hyperglobalization and be fitted for a Golden Straitjacket. Alternatively, governance might seem simple if a great wall could be built surrounding a jurisdiction, prohibiting cross-border interactions and thereby insulating residents from unwanted influences originating in the outside world.

But simplicity is not the only criterion for good decisions. Nor do magic border membranes exist that freely permit beneficial interactions with the outside world yet reliably filter out unwanted influences. Wishful thinking does not foster good choices. Crafting sensible trade-offs is inevitable for good policies.

Recognizing the powerful forces of economic interdependence and the associated benefits of external openness need not be tantamount to forswearing efforts to shape the way that external forces influence events at home. A restricted range of policies may exist that can introduce some degree of differentiation from—and at least a marginal amount of friction with—the outside world.

Such policies can be metaphorically labeled a *separation buffer* (or even *separation fence*) for a nation's borders. Few jurisdictions, especially at the higher vertical level of provinces and nations, have completely disassembled their separation buffers—

nor have the buffers become so porous as to be entirely irrelevant.

A less misleading analogy than either the Golden Straitjacket or a great wall is to regard a nation as a relatively unprotected island in a large and sometimes turbulent ocean. The jurisdiction's institutions are the harbors through which shipping into and out of the island pass. The practical question for the nation's governing authorities is whether the harbors can be modified to function as partially sheltered lagoons. The sea cannot be kept entirely out of the harbors. When storms break out on the open ocean, the harbors and, hence, the entire island are inevitably buffeted. But it may be reasonable to consider building breakwaters around the harbors, to render them less unsafe when storms do occur. Breakwaters have limited effectiveness. But they are better than no protection at all. A cordon sanitaire quarantine protecting a nation from a dangerous health epidemic originating abroad is a health-emergency example.

Analogously, the nation could establish, in effect, "tollhouses" or "boundary markers" pertaining to its borders. With such features in place, the nation could be capable of levying taxes or imposing other restraints on some types of cross-border transactions. "Erosion-control barriers" (for example, language requirements for educational instruction of children) might be devised to inhibit the erosion of indigenous values and institutions by foreign values and institutions.

The components of separation buffers may focus either on the economic and financial dimensions of cross-border interactions or on various aspects of the social-political dimensions. For many nations, most or all dimensions may be significant. Separation buffers require strategic choices designed to favorably influence the external vulnerability of a nation's economy and polity.

Borders and their separation buffers are diverse. Their specific characteristics depend closely on the jurisdictions that they surround. Social norms and social capital differ prominently across the heterogeneous jurisdictions. Divisiveness within and across horizontally defined jurisdictions is commonplace. Externalities occur frequently in conjunction with cross-border transactions and interactions. Correspondingly, public goods issues are entangled with border buffers.

This book highlights cross-border tensions among large nation-state jurisdictions. It focuses on governance issues associated with those tensions. The cross-border aspects have been relatively neglected in public discourse. They have grown increasingly problematic.

But this new salience should not be misinterpreted. It is not true—and it is certainly not my view—that cross-border issues are invariably more significant than intrajurisdiction tensions and governance choices. Sometimes intrajurisdiction difficulties are decidedly more pressing. Great diversity within can override tensions without. When the potential for inner conflicts is great, the likelihood of attaining collective-action compromises of any sort can be diminished. In any case, intrajurisdiction tensions and governance choices tend to be strongly interdependent with those involving outside jurisdictions.

## De Jure Sovereignty and De Facto Autonomy

Nation-states, the dominant jurisdictions on today's planet, do not have a formal top level of governance shared in common. Numerous international institutions and cross-border consultative mechanisms play increasingly significant roles. Yet many of the international institutions are not strong enough to be highly influential. The consultative mechanisms vary from effective to frail. The nation-states, manifested in their national governments, regard themselves as independent "sovereign" entities much more consequential than the international institutions and consultative mechanisms,

The de jure sovereignty of a nation state is defined by a combination of its history and its constitution and laws. But de jure legal sovereignty—juridical independence—in no sense guarantees that a nation will be able, de facto, to prevent external influences from shaping events and decisions taken within its borders. The political processes, institutions, and leaders of individual nations are constrained, often severely, by the actions of other nations' governments and peoples. The external environment actually facing a nation can be much more consequential than its de jure independence. Again, the increasing integration stemming from cross-border spillover erodes the effective autonomy of the individual nation's policies and institutions.

Legally, sovereignty entails mutual recognition among territorial entities that have formal juridical independence. In broader connotations, sovereignty applied to nation-states presumes that each nation will have indigenous authority structures within its geographical territory. It is presumed that those structures will be free from interference by outside actors. De jure sovereignty presumes, in other words, a norm of nonintervention by outsiders in domestic affairs. Domestic political authorities are, in principle, the arbiters of legitimate behavior within the nation's geographical territory.

The residents of a sovereign nation are thus presumed to be free to shape their behavior to their own values and to select their own political arrangements without direct interference from other nations. Similarly, property rights—inherently territorial for most types of assets—are allocated by nation. The so-called global commons, such as outer space and the seabed outside national territorial waters, are exceptions. Each nation is presumed to have sovereign rights for its residents to exploit their property in accordance with the nation's own preferences and policies.[20]

20. The most common connotations of *sovereignty* in the international-relations literature are termed international legal sovereignty or Westphalian sovereignty (named after the Treaty of Westphalia, which was negotiated in

Legal principles and actual constraints, however, markedly diverge. Differences between de facto autonomy and de jure sovereignty are underappreciated, especially by the general public. Even policymakers frequently suffer from illusions about de facto autonomy. Effective autonomy can be weak and limited. De jure sovereignty is invariably an illusory guide to genuine independence of action. Analysis of the trade-off between local autonomy and external openness can easily be confused, but is seldom enlightened, by focusing on de jure legal sovereignty.

Notwithstanding that de jure sovereignty can be overwhelmed by weak de facto autonomy, the prevailing world system of nation-states continues to be predicated on the presumption of de jure sovereignty. The member nations of the system endorse, at least in rhetoric, the norm of nonintervention by external actors in domestic affairs.

Yet *intervention* is another slippery term. Abrogation of nations' de jure legal sovereignty by external actors—something that is commonplace in history—should be separated into two classes. The first includes external interventions that disregard a nation's legal sovereignty and are *harmful* to the welfare of its residents. The other class includes reductions in legal sovereignty that are welcomed by the nation's residents and that *enhance* national welfare.

Power is distributed asymmetrically across nation-states.

---

Europe in 1648). The presumption of political sovereignty for nations is theoretically analogous to the concept of consumer sovereignty for individuals, in which the individual consumer is presumed, other things being equal, to know best his or her own interests and should be able to exercise them freely in a decentralized manner. Westphalian sovereignty is criticized and not invariably observed. For example, the United Nations (UN) at the 2005 World Summit and in later documents (such as the secretary-general's 2009 report) made commitments to a "Responsibility to Protect (R2P)" doctrine that in effect denies the rigid notion of Westphalian sovereignty. The R2P doctrine continues to be the subject of considerable debate.

A strong nation may violate the sovereignty of a weaker nation through coercion—for example, by threatening sanctions unless the weaker nation modifies some aspect of its policies that the strong nation wants changed. Or strong nations may simply impose their will by military force. Such violations of the norm of nonintervention worsen the well-being of most or all of a weaker nation's residents (or at a minimum, aggravate its current political leaders). These interventions simultaneously violate de jure sovereignty and reduce de facto autonomy.

Of course, abrogation of a nation's legal sovereignty accompanied by reduction in *de facto* autonomy due to coercion or military force is viewed by those nations as adverse. Weaker nations, therefore, have been strong proponents of the sovereignty norm of nonintervention. The nations with the greatest political and military power have found it easiest to develop justifications for overriding the principle of legal sovereignty in circumstances where they desire outcomes that conflict with the principle.

Reductions in legal sovereignty that improve well-being for most or all of the residents of a nation are an entirely different matter. A nation open to the rest of the world may decide, wisely, to accept reductions in its de facto autonomy. The resulting benefits can, as noted above, offset costs from erosion of the ability to sustain local values and institutions different from conditions outside the jurisdiction. If the governing authorities of a nation willingly enter into welfare-enhancing arrangements that supersede the principle of legal sovereignty, the departures from the status quo are not well described as "violations."

These welfare-enhancing arrangements are cooperative accords. Were the arrangements not expected to improve welfare, the nation's governing authorities would not voluntarily agree to them. Refraining from the arrangements is an option. Often, a nation may effectively retain the ability to terminate its consent to the arrangements if they do not work out as anticipated. Examples of such arrangements include contractual commitments with other nations and participation in international treaties or conventions. By virtually any criteria for judging the actions of a nation's governing leadership, it can be sensible to override the principle of legal sovereignty by voluntarily entering into such arrangements.

Therefore, when discussing the goals of external openness and local autonomy, the relevant trade-off is between de facto local autonomy and external openness. De jure sovereignty is often irrelevant! Again, a jurisdiction open to the rest of the world may decide, wisely, to accept reductions in its de facto autonomy. The resulting benefits can decisively offset costs from erosion of the ability to emphasize local values, institutions, and economic conditions different from those prevailing outside.[21]

21. Stewart Patrick, *The Sovereignty Wars: Reconciling America with the World* (2017) stresses the same conclusion: "international cooperation need not undermine sovereignty." "The best measure of effective sovereignty is not the absence of foreign entanglements, but indeed the extensiveness of a country's links with the outside world. It is not about steering clear of international attachments, but about steering global forces and events in a positive direction" (quotes from press release).

They drew a circle that shut us out.
Rebels, heretics, foreigners to flout.
With love and patience, we had the wit to win.
We drew a circle that brought them in.

*Edwin Markham, adaptation of "Outwitted," from*
The Shoes of Happiness, and Other Poems *(1913)*

# 3. Localism

## Social Norms, Heterogeneity, and Divisiveness

The notions of identity and belonging are a continuum. A particular individual has a personal identity and a small-group identity shared within a close-at-hand group such as a family or extended family. Some small-group identities (gender, ethnicity, or race) originate at birth; typically, they are not changeable. Individuals also perceive themselves as sharing defined identities that they themselves choose (such as religious organizations, clubs, or political parties). Individuals may share a group identity defined by the geographical jurisdiction in which they reside (such as a neighborhood association or province). Shared identities may extend across the borders of several different jurisdictions and/or upward through vertical layers of a jurisdiction composed of multiple subjurisdictions. Identities of the broadest scope are those associated with nation-states, international institutions, or the world as a whole.

Individuals and groups are defined in part by their various identities. A large jurisdiction typically exhibits, simultaneously, multiple identities. When members of a group have one or more identities in common and assign a high value to sharing them, the group often is described as a "community." A strong community tends to generate social norms and to manifest a social fabric. *Social fabric* is a loose term for the social capital embedded in a community's norms and institutions. Social capital includes shared social networks within which relationships and collective decisions are marked by cooperation, trust, and reciprocity. It is a sociological glue that binds communities or larger societies more closely together. Social capital often entails the provision of public goods for common benefit.

Within a complex jurisdiction, the multiple identities of individuals and groups overlap. The larger the numbers of residents, the greater the scope for internal heterogeneity. Identities and their associated social norms can be consistent and reinforcing. Inconsistencies and conflicts, however, can be commonplace. Governance arrangements for a jurisdiction's decision space are thus significantly influenced by the heterogeneity of the jurisdiction's multiple identities.

Inconsistencies and clashes are prevalent across the geographical borders of a jurisdiction. Such problems also are frequently important within a jurisdiction and, where politically significant, between subjurisdictions.

Despite internal overlaps and conflicts, a jurisdiction with a strong social fabric may reliably be able to hold diverse groupings and communities together. Residents of the jurisdiction can act to support a social fabric that blends diverse identities and norms without demoting or canceling any of them. Because the diverse identities command general loyalty, it is feasible to reach agreed compromises for collective decisions. When a jurisdiction's social fabric is weak, securing accepted agreement on compromise trade-offs can be difficult. At worst, with an unravelling social fabric, effective compromises for the jurisdiction might not exist.[1]

---

1. In extreme cases the very political viability of a jurisdiction and its subjurisdictions may be at stake. Historical examples jump readily to mind where

The most divisive aspects of heterogeneity in identities and norms stem from differences among residents in ethnicity, race, religion, and cultural traditions. Pronounced diversity in these characteristics can promote fractious behavior. Social identities and norms are then critically shaped by the past history of such behavior. Conflictual behavior can inhibit individuals and smaller groups from creating and nurturing more widely shared visions of their identities. Participation within the jurisdiction in more diverse communities might not occur. Broader identifications might be undermined, if not rejected altogether.

For a geographical jurisdiction identified as a nation-state, how much of a *national identity* overlays the combination of identities of the individual groups and communities within the nation? Is a successful blending of the diverse communities feasible without ignoring or severely demoting particular parts of the whole? To be a well-functioning geographical entity, a nation needs some degree of loyalty and patriotism to the geographical entity itself. Indeed, whether such loyalty and patriotism exist—and whether local identities can be cohesively blended into an umbrella identity for the nation as a whole—is a central governance issue. A key task for national political leadership is to nurture such a cohesive blend and channel it in productive directions. When internal identities and norms are conflictual, cohesion may be limited. Nurturing of national loyalty and patriotism is then especially difficult.

---

intraborder tensions and issues within nation-states have been dominant. Recall the Civil War in the United States in 1860–1865, the internal turbulence in Russia in 1917–1920, and the Nigerian civil war over Biafra in 1967–1970. In times closer to the present, think of tensions within the United Kingdom and especially in Northern Ireland, within Middle Eastern nations among internal groups of contrasting Sunni and Shia faiths, and within Belgium between the Dutch-speaking residents of Flanders and French-speaking residents of Wallonia.

## Insiders and Outsiders

An inevitable feature of national patriotism is that citizens feel greater loyalty to fellow residents than to residents of other nations. The identities of own-nation residents tend, first and foremost, to be self-referencing and inward looking. Centripetal forces pull inward. Other nations are outsider localities, peopled by foreigners.

Put starkly, the interests of national residents tilt toward selfishness. Moreover, many residents believe that national interests *should* be selfish.

For individuals, and hence for members of groups or communities, perceptions of shared identity thus implicitly emphasize the borders of the nation. The emphasis is on "we." The antonym for "we" is "they." "They" are the "not us." "We" are insiders. "They" are outsiders.

Racial, ethnic, or religious groups can easily perceive those across their "we" boundaries as outsiders. And almost all groups tend to "otherize" those outside the group boundary. Strong differentiation of group members can foster apprehensions about outsiders and undermine nascent benevolence toward them. Outsiders may be discriminated against. At worst, they may be ostracized.

A poem by Rudyard Kipling captures the nuances:

> *Father and Mother, and Me*
> *And Sister and Auntie say*
> *All the people like us are We,*
> *And everyone else is They.*
> *And They live over the sea,*
> *While We live over the way.*[2]

---

2. Kipling (1926), following the story "A Friend of the Family."

Insider membership in a group or a community typically entails rights and obligations not shared with outsiders. Such rights and obligations are part of social capital. They constitute a kind of mutual insurance contract. The responsibility to help other insiders and a reciprocal right to expect help from them in return are a social and ethical component of membership. Such special rights and obligations are shared with insiders with whom one shares propinquity (such as kinship or geographical proximity). Insiders are virtually defined as having relatively greater rights and responsibilities than outsiders.

Because of shared insider rights and obligations, the members of a group or community naturally accord priority to advancing insider interests. Their collective social identity rests on "belonging"—on sharing a rootedness in family, ethnic, racial, religious, or ideological identities. The "we" social identity can easily lead the members to presume "my group first" or "my community first." The collective attitude promotes, either intentionally or inadvertently, own values and own interests. Sometimes the social identity can be overtly discriminatory: Insiders may perceive the strength of the group or community as partially dependent on excluding outsiders.

An inward-looking perspective—an identity with, loyalty to, and even selfishness about one's own community and nation—embodies *communitarian* values and behavior. If instead residents manifest some degree of identity with and loyalty to nonresident outsiders, the perspective drifts toward values and behavior that are *cosmopolitan.*

Communitarian insiders care more about their own neighborhood, their own community, their own province—indeed their own nation—than about outsider, foreign localities. Proximity in distance and propinquity of relationships lead naturally to a focus on "us" and local well-being as opposed to concerns about "them." Insider responsibilities and reciprocal expectations from other insiders are a significant component of "us" membership. For example, insiders have greater willingness to pay taxes and devote resources to other insiders when the recipients are rooted participants in local communities and the home nation. The more homogeneous the insider residents are, the stronger the likely emphasis on "us" is.

Insider thinking, of course, varies by type and degree. Extremist insiders might give no weight at all to the views and well-being of foreigners. Other insiders, less extreme, can be labeled *localist*.

Key decisionmakers for a nation—policymakers—are especially sensitive to differentiation of insiders from foreigners. The decisionmakers are acutely aware that local governance is politically accountable to home citizens and residents. With home residents deeply rooted in local values and institutions, policymakers must judge outcomes primarily by whether the home polity, economy, and culture do well or poorly. Their decisions, driven by the interests of local constituencies, must be unabashedly national—and, typically, selfish.

Because home policy decisions give greater weight to the well-being of home residents than of outsiders, most insiders support maintenance of some buffering at the nation's borders. Consequently, home policy similarly is driven to focus on decisions about the separation buffers associated with the borders. For example, policymakers are forced to address whether prudent and cost-effective measures exist for protecting home insiders from the unwanted movement of goods, financial funds, and cultural traditions across the national borders. The most controversial issues of all are raised in regard to the cross-border movements of people. To what degree should a nation's residents welcome or restrict the movement of nonresident foreigners in and out of the nation?

Individuals' views are of course diverse. Not every home resident emphasizes communitarian localist attitudes. A minority may explicitly espouse an outward-looking cosmopolitan perspective. Such individuals or groups may wish to counter what they perceive as an excessive focus on national identity. After all, residents of a single nation are ineluctably participants in a wider world community. A nation must on occasion cooperate with other nations to further its own separate objectives.

Hence some degree of thoughtful cosmopolitanism is rational on purely selfish grounds. A prudent openness to the outside brings numerous net benefits that selfishly raise the well-being of insiders. A second motive likewise encourages interactions with outsiders. For humanitarian reasons alone, local residents may wish to relate to and help outsiders. Humanitarian considerations can be especially significant when outsiders suffer from adverse developments such as political turbulence or natural disasters. Humanitarian perspectives also underly efforts to ameliorate poverty and other disadvantages experienced by outsiders.

Notwithstanding the natural tendency toward insider selfishness, the propensity to otherize the not-us can possibly be overridden by compassion and generosity. The shared sense of "we" does not invariably divide group members from everyone else. Heterogeneity of values and backgrounds among insiders can encourage or even celebrate within-group pluralism and thereby also nurture openness to foreigners. Shared social capital can be developed by collective benevolence.

The final lines of Kipling's poem allude to such contradictory nuances:

> *All good people agree,*
> *And all good people say,*
> *All nice people, like Us, are We*
> *And everyone else is They:*
> *But if you cross over the sea,*
> *Instead of over the way,*
> *You may end by (think of it!) looking on We*
> *    As only a sort of They!*[3]

---

3. Ibid.

Therefore, even when insiders emphasize national identity and national loyalty, they can advocate a blending of some cosmopolitanism with their communitarian localism. Some residents may be recognized as part of a group or community yet perceived by other members (and by themselves) as dissenters from the prevalent social identity. Such individuals, because they do not fully share the prevalent social identity, may be de facto outsiders even though they are formally insiders.[4]

Looking far enough into the future, national policymakers might even begin to sense a nascent identity for a wider community of multiple nation-states. With sufficient commonality of interests, enhanced cooperation combined with prudent openness can facilitate better outcomes for many nations combined.[5]

## Simultaneously Looking Inward and Outward

How the variety of insider identities and decision spaces can— or cannot—be successfully blended is a patchwork achievement unique to each individual nation. The patchwork incorporates attitudes and behaviors that can range on a spectrum all the way

---

4. Steven Weisman, *The Great Tradeoff: Confronting Moral Conflicts in the Era of Globalization* (2016) analyzes at length the trade-off between communitarianism and cosmopolitanism (see especially chapters 9 and 10).

5. Subjurisdictions within a multilayer jurisdiction, and higher-level jurisdictions themselves, typically have their own social identities. Jurisdictional and subjurisdictional identities raise additional issues. How meaningful to resident citizens are the jurisdiction's borders? Heterogeneities and divisiveness across jurisdictions pose additional obstacles to collective-action decisions. To what degree does the perceived identity of a jurisdiction welcome the movement of nonresident foreigners in and out of the jurisdiction? Can foreigners share many aspects of the jurisdiction's cultures and traditions? Are foreigners (the not-us "others") viewed in a hostile light or a roughly equivalent light compared to insider citizens? Later parts of the book return to these questions.

from extreme inward-looking localism to the opposite endpoint of unquestioned cosmopolitanism.

When inward-looking localism dominates, internal groups and communities are all-important. Creating workable consensuses among the various groups and subjurisdictions is a higher priority than anything else. For those with an ultracosmopolite perspective, attitudes are entirely different. The identities, social norms, and institutions outside the nation's borders may have at least as much salience as those inside. Rights and privileges of outsiders are not sharply differentiated from those of insiders. A rooted geographical grounding may even be absent altogether.

The notion of geographical rootedness, of belonging to a geographical jurisdiction or subjurisdiction, has been emphasized by David Goodhart. An extreme localist is a rigid "somewhere," embedded in local groups and communities. Somewheres belong at home, ascribing their identities to their groups and locales. They may emphasize the mutual obligations of kinship. Somewheres may be ill at ease with changes in economic, social, and cultural institutions. They may be especially uncomfortable with free movement across the borders and especially the cross-border migration of people.

In contrast, an "anywhere" is Goodhart's classification for individuals who are less, or perhaps not at all, geographically rooted. Anywheres are not wedded to narrow definitions of their groups. Their identities are associated predominantly with traits that are portable across borders. For example, independently of residency, an anywhere might give priority to education, job experiences, and nonlocal cultural traditions. Anywheres tend to be at ease with economic, social, and cultural change. They are more willing to move across borders to locations with greater opportunities.

Individuals and groups in the middle of the spectrum, expressing perspectives about geographical belonging that are neither localist-somewhere nor cosmopolitan-anywhere, are labeled by Goodhart as "in-betweeners."[6]

Extreme localists can be unreservedly self-referencing and selfish. They believe and act narrowly as somewheres. Somewheres tend to lack empathy for a cosmopolitan mentality. Extreme anywheres tend to be zealously outward looking. They manifest ultracosmopolite views. They have little empathy for the geographical rootedness of the fervent somewheres. In-betweeners, eschewing both extremes, mix the somewheres' inward-looking attitudes with those of outward-looking anywheres.

Local autonomy and external openness are each, taken alone, a valid goal. Yet the extreme versions of each—self-sufficient autarky and untrammeled openness—are starkly incompatible. A trade-off combination, a center of gravity between the two goals, is a necessity.

A home community (or the home nation as a whole) risks adverse net effects when excessive localism emphasizes merely communitarian, inward-looking attitudes. Particular individuals

---

6. The distinctions emphasized by Goodhart are in *The Road to Somewhere: The Populist Revolt and the Future of Politics* (Hurst, 2017). Jonathan Freedland published a review of Goodhart's book in *The Guardian* (March 22, 2017, modified November 29, 2017), where he summarized the argument with an emphasis on the situation in the United Kingdom at the time of the Brexit referendum in 2017. "The key faultline in Britain and elsewhere now separates those who come from Somewhere—rooted in a specific place or community, usually a small town or in the countryside, socially conservative, often less educated—and those who could come from Anywhere: footloose, often urban, socially liberal and university educated." Goodhart cites polling evidence to show that, at the time, somewheres made up roughly half the U.K. population, anywheres accounted for 20 percent to 25 percent, with the rest classified as "in-betweeners." The somewheres/anywheres distinction correlates strongly with the leave/remain divide in the Brexit referendum (albeit the victory margin for the voting was a narrow 52 percent to 48 percent). David Brooks applied Goodhart's distinctions to the United States in a *New York Times* column of November 10, 2017.

or small groups will no doubt be extreme localists. Such extreme attitudes cannot be prevented altogether. But at best, excessive localism should not dominate an average of jurisdiction views.

Moderate localism gives balanced weight to the particular strengths of a home locality. When collective social identity and loyalty exist, they naturally emphasize "us," nurtured by loyalty and patriotism. But localism also needs to be skillful and responsible, guiding the home locality to a healthy, stable engagement with the world economy and world polity. An overly exclusive and selfish emphasis on a nation's "us" can undermine stable interactions with the "them" of neighboring nations.

Yes, just as a group naturally emphasizes "my group comes first," a nation instinctively manifests the view "my nation first." Yet for the center of gravity for all views taken together, it is dangerous for "my nation first" to drift mindlessly toward "my nation only." Localist tendencies need to be restrained from going too far, thereby incurring the high costs that can result from yearning to create a barrier to insulate a home nation from external influences.

Insider preoccupation can cause damage by unwisely alienating foreigners. Valuable compassion for and cooperation with foreigners can be undermined. Even local dissent from skeptical insiders can be unwisely suppressed. At its worst, aggressive localism can morph into tribal nativism, narrowly local populism, and unabashed nationalism. It can become xenophobia if many local residents aggressively assert "my nation first—full stop, no qualifications."

Excessive emphasis on outward-looking cosmopolitanism is not good for the home nation either. Untrammeled openness with no buffers at the border—hyperglobalization—could make the nation acutely vulnerable to the rest of the world. Such vulnerability could in turn generate high gross costs, the burden of which could fall especially heavily on home residents that are least able to adjust to hyperglobalization.

Excessively cosmopolitan views are not likely to be sustainable in most nations because they cannot garner widespread political support. If adverse redistribution effects for some home residents are ignored in governance choices, political sustainability becomes especially difficult.

Quandaries about belonging are symbolized by concepts such as *family* and *citizen*. Who is a family member? Who is a citizen? If every individual in all world locations were to be deemed a member of a world family, then all individuals might be said to have coequal status. No person would belong to a family except in a bland rhetorical sense. The traditional kinship notion of family would be so inflated that it might seem virtually empty. Analogously, if *citizen* were deemed to refer to every individual in the entire world community, the concept of citizen would drift toward having little practical specific meaning. If one's neighbors see themselves merely as citizens of the world as a whole, they are open to the assertion that in practice they are citizens of nowhere.[7]

The ultracosmopolite stance is thus no less politically fraught than excessive localism. To quote the journalist James Traub, "The answer to xenophobia cannot be unqualified xenophilia."

Inescapably, a balance must be crafted. An exclusively cosmopolitan approach is patently inappropriate for appraising the average well-being of residents. No predominantly localist approach makes good sense either. To emphasize the point again,

---

7. Kwame Anthony Appiah, as quoted by Steven Weisman, observes starkly that "cosmopolitan judgment requires us to feel about everyone in the world what we feel about our literal neighbors but this does not mean that distant sufferers have the same grip on our sympathies as our nearest and dearest. . . . Whatever basic obligations are to the poor far away, they cannot be enough, I believe, to trump my concerns for my family, my friends, my country nor can an argument that every life matters require me to be indifferent to the fact that one of those lives is mine." See Weisman (2016, p.141) and Appiah (2006, pp. 157–158, 165).

yes, it is appropriate to place a relatively larger weight on the well-being of local residents than of foreigners. But an excessive weight on localism harms the nation.

An in-betweener temperament needs to dominate the mentalities of the vocal somewheres and the enthusiastic anywheres. On average, residents should look inward *and they should simultaneously look outward.* Policy choices for governance units at both lower-level jurisdictions and, above all, for entire nations must balance the demands of both perspectives.

The larger the proportion of a jurisdiction's residents who share an in-betweener temperament, the more likely it is that governance choices can craft a politically sustainable trade-off.[8]

---

8. I am not suggesting that crafting a balance between localism and cosmopolitanism is straightforward, nor that a clear line separates "good localism" from "bad localism." An essay by James Meek perceptively illustrates the difficulties. "At the communitarian end—the part of the liberal spectrum where I like to think I reside—there's a tendency to assume that 'good' localism (the ideal of the 'thriving local community', locally sourced food, the preservation of vernacular local architecture and traditional local landscapes) can be neatly separated from 'bad' localism (hostility to immigrants and new ways of doing things). It can't. While writing about the closure of a Cadbury's factory in the west of England, I was pleased to find there was still one small family chocolatier left in Bristol, producing chocolates by hand in an old atelier in the city centre. My heart sank when the artisan patriarch launched into a tirade about how most of the children born at the local maternity hospital were born to foreigners. I liked his localism, until suddenly I didn't. Writing about Britain's housing crisis, I spent hours with an elderly resident of a council block in Bethnal Green, a fourth-generation East Ender. Eventually, after many fascinating stories about her life, she said: 'The majority of people in here now are immigrants. Would there be a housing crisis if we hadn't let so many people in? Now the white English are a minority.' I liked her localism, and then, suddenly, not so much. Who was the more nativist here? Her? Or me, being so pleased at first that I'd found somebody whose personal history in that place reached back so deep?" Meek (October 11, 2018).

Something there is that doesn't love a wall,
That sends the frozen-ground-swell under it,
And spills the upper boulders in the sun.
. . . I let my neighbor know beyond the hill;
And on a day we meet to walk the line
And set the wall between us once again. . . .
He will not go behind his father's saying,
He says again, Good fences make good neighbors.

*Robert Frost,* **Mending Wall**

# 4. Border Buffers

Separation buffers at the border of a jurisdiction can be justified when they help to promote a responsible balance between localism and external openness. A jurisdiction may want to try to protect itself from outside-originating disruptions when home residents and home governing authorities have no direct control over the disruptions. An alternative rationalization is to nurture some of the jurisdiction's own idiosyncratic characteristics and try to prevent erosion from outside influences. And local residents—represented by their governing authorities—may selfishly seek to promote their own well-being. If coupled with little or no regard for how local policy actions influence the well-being of outsiders, this third justification can lead to border buffers that undermine a responsible balance between localism and openness.

Persuasive rationales for separation buffers at the border aim to rectify externalities and market failures (chapter 2). But externalities affecting whom? The perceptions of externality problems as seen by local residents are likely to differ from the perceptions of outsiders (chapter 3). Further, if border buffers are used as hostile weapons by an aggressive jurisdiction (chapter 7), the pretense that externalities and market failures are the underlying rationale is self-evidently false.

How, then, should a jurisdiction proceed in establishing separation buffers?

## General Guidelines

Seen from the perspective of a local (home) jurisdiction, metaphors invoking the functions desired for border buffers are multiple. They include breakwaters shielding against external storms; cordons sanitaires protecting against epidemics originating abroad; tollhouses that tax, subsidize, or otherwise influence cross-border transactions; and gatekeeping concierges that monitor and collect information about cross-border flows. Among the important issues are the behaviors, transactions, and investments of foreigners inside the home nation, as well as of foreigners who reside outside. For example, what restraints, if any, may be needed to influence or modify foreigners' activities?

To maintain successful border buffers, a jurisdiction must have an administrative governance structure that is responsible for developing and implementing appropriate policies. The priority governance functions include systematic monitoring and analytical oversight of cross-border transactions. A gathering of relevant information and statistical data is a basic requirement for sound policies, regulations, and procedures. Whatever border buffers are selected for implementation should also be backstopped with periodically updated evaluations of whether existing buffers need to adapt to changed circumstances.

The relevant governance institutions differ by nation and by types of activity. Separate ministries or agencies typically monitor trade and nonfinancial service transactions, together with the implementation of associated regulations and standards.

The central bank and finance or treasury ministries typically are responsible for border buffers dealing with issues related to financial systems and financial services. Monitoring and control aspects of cross-border movement, including customs enforcement and data collection, involve still other bodies.

The following are some general guidelines for a jurisdiction's design and use of border buffers. For simplicity, the wording presumption here is that the jurisdictions are nation-states.[1] These guidelines are unabashedly normative. And they are, of course, controversial.

**The home nation should be a member of, and in good standing with, the wider world community of nations.** Increasing integration across borders pervasively influences all nations in the global polity and economy. All nations experience heightened pressures to participate in collective actions to address common problems. The gradual, episodic drift toward international collective action requires occasional participation by virtually every single nation. Therefore, planning and implementation of home governance must at times defer to cooperation with other jurisdictions in the wider world community. To facilitate reaping the rewards of external openness, the home nation must be a respected member, in good standing, of that community. If deference is not given to cooperative participation, harmful frictions and losses to home well-being can result.

**The well-being of home residents should be a top priority but not an exclusive focus; wise home governance cannot be impervious to well-being outside the nation.** This guideline distills earlier conclusions. Tilting to give greater weight to the

---

1. Analogous guidelines apply in a multilayer jurisdiction to lower-level subjurisdictions—with, when needed, appropriate adjustments at the lower levels for governing institutions, relevant constraints, and the allocation of authorities between the upper-level and lower-level subjurisdictions.

well-being of home residents than to the well-being of outsiders is the essence of localism, of keeping some distinction between "us" and "them." But there exists a dangerous risk of overdoing that tilting by indulging in excess selfishness.

A corollary is that, when possible, home governance should select border buffers and other policy measures that significantly benefit home residents but do not cause significant harm to outsiders. In particular, buffers should not be implemented where the harm to foreign outsiders greatly exceeds gains to local residents. It would be counterproductive to implement border buffers that harm foreign entities merely because they are foreigners.

These recommendations rest on the venerable idea of, when possible, "do no harm." This no-harm guideline aspires to limit actions by some in order to prevent harm to others.[2] When border buffers avoid creating situations where foreign harms will significantly exceed home gains, the world system of nations tends on balance to experience "positive-sum" gains. The larger the net positive-sum gains are for the world, the higher the probability that the world system can function smoothly and beneficially for its participants. Home governance should definitely be wary of measures that benefit the home nation at the expense of large losses to outsiders.

**Home governing authorities should, in advance, evaluate likely reactions of foreign jurisdictions to prospective changes in home policies.** This guideline is based on the rationale that when border buffers adversely influence outsiders, it can induce reactive policies by foreign authorities intended to offset harm to their residents. Adverse foreign reactions are especially pos-

---

2. John Stuart Mill articulated this dictum (in Latin, *primum non nocere)* in *On Liberty* (1859), where he argued that the only purpose for which power can be rightfully exercised over any member of a civilized community against his will is to prevent harm to others. An equivalent was stated as early as 1789 in France's Declaration of the Rights of Man and of the Citizen.

sible when home decisions are introduced provocatively and stridently. Offsetting foreign policies, if they undo the hoped-for benefits of prospective home policies, can leave all jurisdictions worse off. Hence home border policies that produce only transitory gains prior to foreign reactions should be selected very warily, if at all. More generally, home measures should always be chosen in light of how other nations may choose their policies. Analogous recommendations pertain to how a home jurisdiction should respond to foreign policies that may be harmful to some or all home residents.

**Home authorities should carefully evaluate their reactions to unwanted policies implemented by foreign jurisdictions and avoid tit-for-tat self-defeating interactions with foreign authorities.** An important aspect of good home decisions is a thoughtful differentiation of how foreign policy actions and home reactions affect home residents in transitory short-run ways versus effects that persist over a longer run. Especially over the longer run, co-operative agreements across jurisdictions can potentially yield mutually large net gains. All jurisdictions have strong incentives to cooperate fairly and to assure agreement partners that their commitments can be trusted.[3]

**The monitoring of cross-border transactions conducted by home governance should pay attention to not merely the aggregate effects on the nation as a whole, but also disaggregated information for particular groups or subgroups of residents.** For home residents for whom external openness causes negative net benefits, home governance should carefully consider compensa-

3. When reading a draft of this paragraph, a political science colleague remarked that an important goal of political analysis is to identify which behaviors are beneficially cooperative in facilitating agreement, how to define guidelines for possible defection by some members, and how cooperating members should appropriately respond to plans or actions by defecting members.

tion and redistributive measures that can cushion such adverse consequences. Without such compensatory measures, the nation may not be able to sustain an existing compromise between localism and external openness.

**Home governance should be wary of implementing border buffers that strongly favor only a small subset of home citizens, especially if most home citizens do not benefit at all or are adversely affected.** Controversial distributive consequences can crucially influence outcomes. Measures with narrowly distributed domestic effects are more easily influenced by particular local interests (or even captured through corruption of governance processes). Protection of narrowly defined vested interests often does not generate net benefits for an entire nation.[4]

**When home governance provides public goods that are financed by local tax revenues, home residents should have a presumptive priority over foreign residents in enjoying access to those public goods.** When home-generated public goods are created and financed by home governing authorities, some complications are inevitable. Many issues about access to home public goods are delicate. Policies may even need to distinguish between local residents who are home citizens, local residents who are not home citizens, and foreigners who are temporarily located in the home nation.[5] Home localists are likely to believe that home citizens should enjoy preferred access relative to foreigners who are temporarily or permanently inside the home nation. The preference for restricting the consumption of home public goods to

4. Protective subsidies for sugar production in the United States are a textbook illustration of why this guideline can be important. The overall well-being of U.S. residents and that of foreign sugar growers wanting to export sugar to the United States are both harmed by protective measures that benefit U.S. sugar growers.

5. Foreigners currently located in the home nation who aspire to become permanent home residents and citizens raise additional complications.

local citizens is strongest when the public goods require exclusive financing via home-generated tax revenues.

**Governing authorities should choose buffer policies that are conditioned by the details of the supposed externalities and market failures being addressed.** This guideline merits emphasis because, again, the underlying rationales for most buffers is to rectify externalities and market failures. The guideline applies both to home authorities and those of outside jurisdictions. Appropriate border buffers depend on the particulars of externalities and the particulars of markets. "Markets" in this generalization are a combination of market arrangements within a jurisdiction considering the buffer and market arrangements located outside the jurisdiction's border.

Because circumstances and conditions across nations are so higgledy-piggledy, the specifics of border buffers cannot typically be designed in common. Effective uniformity across national jurisdictions often is neither possible nor desirable. Generally applicable specifics, especially when simplified, do not exist. Adaptation to localist pressure points and tensions is essential. True, international cooperation in designing collaborative norms and agreements, which in turn nurture cross-border understandings, should play a central role (more on that below). But variations in local cultures, customs, religions, and political histories inevitably require diversity in border buffers. For all jurisdictions, not least for nation-states, the familiar adage applies: *different strokes for different folks.*

The ability of a nation to craft a successful balance between localism and openness–successful in the sense of effectual as well as internationally responsible—depends in part on the size of the nation as well as its particular characteristics. Other things being equal, larger nations (those with greater populations, bigger land areas, or both) may have greater scope than smaller nations for accommodating and reconciling divergences in localist idiosyncrasies. However, another generalization works in the opposite direction. Some forms of domestic tensions are more probable in heterogeneous jurisdictions than in homogeneous ones. For those tensions, larger jurisdictions might have greater difficulties in identifying consensus.

Governing authorities confront difficult problems when designing buffers to influence cross-border transactions in capital (monies and investments) and cross-border trade in goods and services. But movement of people in and out of a nation is frequently the most difficult challenge of all in establishing suitable separation fences. The rest of this chapter focuses on specifics about cross-border transactions in goods, services, and finance. Buffers for the cross-border migration of peoples are discussed in chapter 5.

## Border Buffers for Goods, Services, and Financial Transactions

Establishing border buffers entails swimming upstream. That is because organization of economic activity in a unified market free of impediments can offer powerful gains, including increased specialization from comparative advantage, larger economies of scale, and heightened competition. Goods and factors of production can move to locations where they are most valued and most efficiently used.

The introduction of border buffers involves surrendering potential benefits of greater external openness. Well-designed buffers achieve their localist goals best when, cautiously and carefully, they surrender as little as possible of the potential gains of openness.

Box 4-1 shows the types of border buffers most commonly applied to transactions in goods and nonfinancial services.

Tariffs are widely imposed on most classes of imports. Taxes might also be imposed on various exports (though less often in recent decades). Quotas and other nontariff barriers are widely used as substitutes or supplements for tariffs. Quotas are more

BOX 4-1. **Border Buffers for Cross-Border Transactions in Goods and Nonfinancial Services**

**Imports of Goods and Nonfinancial Services into Home Nation**

- Tariffs (taxes, ad valorem or specific)
- Quotas (maximum amount permitted into nation)
    *Sometimes associated with a required license*
- Other pecuniary charges imposed by nontariff barriers
    *Local content requirements*
    *Not able to import without a home nation approved license*
- Prohibitions on particular foreign goods for reasons of safety standards or other regulations
- Other restraints on imports into home nation

**Exports of Goods and Nonfinancial Services from Home Nation**

- Taxes or duties imposed on home nation exports (different from taxes or duties imposed by foreign governing authorities on the home nation's exports to the foreign nation)
- Subsidies provided by home governing authorities to permit cheaper exports to foreigners

**Collection and Reporting of Statistical Data, and Monitoring of Associated Problems (both for imports and exports, goods as well as nonfinancial services)**

- Design and monitoring of Mutual Recognition Agreements (MRAs) and associated conformity assessments

blunt instruments; they are often used to achieve specific objectives for reducing or managing particular imports. Nontariff barriers are also associated with safety and design regulations for particular products.

The dominant motives behind the imposition of tariffs, quotas, and nontariff barriers are to reduce foreign competition, encourage or safeguard domestic activities, induce consumption of home goods rather than imports, and thereby protect local producers and workers. By reducing foreign competition, the border buffers can be justified as protecting "infant industries" and enhancing "import substitution industrialization." For many nations the goal of generating revenues to support public expenditures by governing authorities has also been a dominant motivation for tariffs or export taxes. Shipments of most types of goods and nonfinancial services crossing international borders are subject to duty and tax assessment by the importing country's governing authorities.[6]

A key attribute of border buffers is to differentiate transactions between domestic and foreign residents from transactions among only domestic residents. Prohibitions are sometimes placed on particular foreign goods because of safety standards or other home regulatory objectives. Subsidies are sometimes provided to local producers to permit cheaper, larger-volume exports to foreigners. A major complication of cross-border transactions is the prevalence of intrafirm relationships among domestic and foreign-based parts of multinational corporations, the so-called value chains in the production of manufactured goods.[7]

Box 4-2 lists types of border buffers imposed on or differentially influencing cross-border financial transactions. Most of these buffers are supervisory and prudential regulations, typically different for banks and nonbank financial institutions. For example, reserve requirements on the deposit liabilities of banks' domestic offices can be set differently for foreigners versus local residents. Requirements can differ for capital ratios and liquidity-coverage ratios, and limitations on various asset positions. Taxes on the profits of financial institutions or regulations mandating

---

6. Tariffs or quotas on exports of particular goods conserve those products for home use and thereby encourage local consumption. Motives for taxing exports include the raising of revenue.

7. For discussion of cross-border value chains in the production of manufactured products by multinational corporations, see Richard Baldwin, *The Great Convergence: Information Technology and the New Globalization* (2016).

BOX 4-2. Border Buffers for Cross-Border
Financial Transactions

**Supervisory and Prudential Regulations—typically different for banks and nonbanks**

- Capital requirements (minimum limits on capital as percentage of asset categories)
- Liquidity coverage ratios
- Reserve requirements on liabilities
- Limits on various asset positions
    *Example:* open (net) position in assets denominated in foreign currencies as a percentage of total capital
- Tax rates on profits income; tax withholding on interest payments
    *Example:* withholding tax on flows of financial funds into home nation
- Periodic reviews and evaluation of balance sheets and management
- Operation of payments systems, and registration and security procedures
- Other microprudential regulations, standards, and guidelines
- Other macroprudential regulations, standards, and guidelines

**Ownership Requirements and Limitations**

- Different for banks and nonbank financial institutions

**Regulations for Monetary-Policy Control Set by Home Central Bank**

- Different for banks and nonbank financial institutions

**Collection and Reporting of Statistical Data, and Monitoring of Associated Problems**

withholding of customers' earnings could depend on the cross-border features of balance sheets. Special regulations may apply to the cross-border features of the operation of asset exchanges or payments flows. Supervisory and prudential regulations for financial institutions can be set at levels that are more stringent than average, with the objective of reducing risks in the home financial system. Alternatively, the prudential standards could be set at levels that are less stringent than average, hoping to induce foreign financial institutions to relocate their activities to home locations.

Requirements and limitations may also be imposed differentially on the ownership of home-located financial institutions depending on whether they are held and managed by domestic or foreign entities. For example, home governing authorities might require special approval for large investments by foreign-owned entities in home-located financial institutions. Additionally, there can be possible financial regulations and procedures associated with the conduct of the home central bank over its general monetary policies for the home financial system.

Details of border buffers in the financial system can be complicated. One underlying motive for many prudential standards and regulations is to reduce home vulnerability to shocks originating from outside. But the still-broader motive is to protect the stability of the financial system from disruptions, whether originating either at home or abroad.

Consider a prudential restraint requiring individual banks to limit their open (net) position in foreign currencies to no more than a modest percentage of their total capital. That restraint may be not so much a border buffer per se, but rather a component of the macroprudential oversight regime in which supervisors require financial institutions to hold minimum capital in relation to their total balance sheets. A similar example is the imposition of reserve requirements on the short-term liabilities to foreign depositors and investors in the domestic offices of financial institutions. The rate of reserve requirement on these liabilities to foreigners could be set higher than the rate on similar liabilities to domestic residents. The underlying motives here could include both the general protection of financial stability and the particular goal of moderating the potential disruption from skittish foreign investment. Imposition of a withholding tax on inflows of foreign investors' funds into home financial institutions would be a further illustration of a controversial attempt to dampen the volatile capital flows of skittish foreign investors.

Yet another complication merits emphasis. Home norms, regulations, and standards impose constraints on local producers of products and services. These controls include, for example, product safety or design standards, labor safety and other working condition standards, air and water pollution requirements, and product innovation and patent regulations.

Local home standards and regulations may often differ from standards and regulations enforced in foreign nations. Foreign competitors may find it too expensive to meet local standards. If they are more stringent than those in foreign nations, the local standards can act much like tariffs or quotas, effectively narrowing or even eliminating foreign competition for domestic producers.

Differences between home and foreign labor-market conditions can attract controversy. Points of contention may include requirements for minimum wages to be paid, limitations on hours worked, age restrictions on employment, and procedures for resolving disputes between workers and supervisors. If local standards are more stringent, local producers may complain they are forced to compete unfairly against the lax labor regulations abroad; workers in foreign jurisdictions may complain they are maltreated relative to home workers. Opposite attitudes may generate controversy when standards for home working conditions are less stringent than those abroad.

Local home and foreign restrictions may well differ for standards and regulations influencing environmental protection of air and water supplies. Home governance may impose tighter restrictions on emission of pollutants than in foreign nations where such restrictions are absent altogether. Alternatively, perhaps home restrictions might be even more lax than those abroad. Either way the differences have implications for competitive equity between the home and foreign nations.

Or consider regulations pertaining to foreign firms or individuals that are resident in or carrying out transactions with home firms and individuals. Ownership rights in domestic property might be tilted to favor home residents. Foreign entities may have to get special approval from local governing authorities to make significant investments in home firms or other property.

Such interactions between home locals and foreigners related to domestic standards and regulations are not, strictly speaking, issues about border buffers per se. But they can cause analogous tensions and thorny discussions about level playing fields (see below). Box 4-3 indicates how domestic standards and regulations can interact with border buffers.

Within a home nation, many other norms, practices, and policies that are noneconomic and cultural also have implications for cross-border interactions. Box 4-4 is a reminder of their potential significance.

For instance, local residents typically have preferences about the languages appropriate for official and public discourse. One specific language might be specified for exclusive use in official documents and on official occasions. Strong predilections may exist about which languages should be used in local schools. Such choices may not be controversial with foreigners (even foreigners who are resident locally in the home nation). But the choices are reflections of the predominant cultural norms.

Cultural norms are also strongly reflected in the content and social behaviors taught in local schools and other institutions for the education of children. The same is true for a majority of local

BOX 4-3. **Interactions of Border Buffers with Domestic Standards and Regulations**

**Domestic Norms, Regulations, and Standards That Influence Foreign Competition**
- Product safety or design standards with which imported foreign products must comply
- Standards and regulations for labor requirements and compensation
- Local standards for environmental requirements
- Regulation of patents, innovations, and grants of preference
- Standards and regulations governing human rights, including differentiations (if any) for local citizens versus locally resident foreigners
- Design and monitoring of Mutual Recognition Agreements" (MRAs) and conformity assessments

**Labor and Working Conditions**
- Limitations on hours worked
- Requirements for minimum wages to be paid
- Procedures for resolving disputes between workers and supervisors

**Home Nation Production, Commercial, and Other Economic Facilities Owned and Managed by Foreigners**
- Ownership rights of foreigners versus domestic residents
- Design and monitoring of Good Manufacturing Practices (GMPs)

**Collection and Reporting of Statistical Data, and Monitoring of Associated Problems**

cultural activities not specifically educational. And attitudes and behaviors are strongly shaped by ethnic identities and traditions.

Religious traditions and practices within a nation might be especially important for influencing cross-border interactions. Such influences reflect the degree of homogeneity or heterogene-

BOX 4-4. **Noneconomic Home Nation Norms, Practices, and Policies Shaping Cross-Border Interactions**

**Spoken and Written Language**
- Preferences for use of specific "official" language in public occasions and documents
- Preferences for language(s) to be used in school for education of children

**Education and Cultural Norms**
- Guidelines, curricula, and procedures to be used in local schools and other institutions for children
- Local procedures encouraging particular cultural norms, practices, and activities

**Local Cultural and Ethnic Characteristics**
- Guidelines other than language for use of cultural and national traditions for the education of children in school
- Standards and regulations governing human rights, including differentiations (if any) for local citizens versus locally resident foreigners

**Religious Traditions and Degree of Diversity**
- Some traditions and practices encouraged locally more than others?
- Regulations affecting the boundaries between religious-organization events and the activities of public-sector institutions

**Requirements for Collection and Reporting of Statistical Data**
- More extensive and stringent for foreign entities than for local entities?

**Provision of Social Insurance and Other Public Goods**
(Available more readily, or even only, to citizens who pay taxes for their support? Exceptions to this guideline?)
- Social insurance (health care, retirement support)
- Support for fees at educational institutions
- Public libraries and public parks

ity in religious beliefs. Some nations may domestically encourage the traditions and practices of one particular religion. Internal home regulations might affect the boundaries between domestic religious-organization events and the activities of public-sector institutions.

Each nation is likely to require that firms and other entities located within the home nation but owned and managed by foreigners should at the very least adhere to all local laws and regulations to which home residents must adhere. Consider the example of data reporting requirements. Entities owned by foreigners should at least conform to the minimum submissions required by home authorities. The reporting requirements for locally resident foreign entities might well be even more extensive and stringent.

The provision of social insurance (such as retirement support and health care) and other public goods to foreign residents who are locally resident in the home nation is potentially contentious if those residents do not pay local taxes to cover the costs of provision. Remember that, as a general guideline for border buffers recommends, when home governance provides public goods that are financed by local tax revenues, local residents should have a presumptive priority over foreign residents in enjoying access to those public goods. But the presence within the home nation of noncitizen foreigners, especially if they are long-standing residents, of course creates complications. Can health care humanely be denied to severely ill noncitizens? Should noncitizens be ineligible for lower fees at educational institutions? Would it not be impractical to ask noncitizens to pay to go to public libraries and public parks that are free for local citizens?

Sometimes it is reasonable to stipulate different regulations, procedures, and standards for foreigners than those pertaining to local citizens. Sometimes it is reasonable to establish regulations, procedures, and standards that differentiate between local citizens and locally resident foreigners. But in other cases, such discrimination is not reasonable or practical.

As illustrated here, border buffers necessarily reflect myriad ways in which local home norms and practices are not identical with the norms and practices applying to foreigners. Acceptance and celebration of that diversity can undergird smooth social relationships within nations and in cross-border communications. If instead the diversity is not accepted and becomes sharp or fractious, social relationships are much less smooth both at home and abroad.

What overall attitude should guide a home nation's authorities for establishing and managing the nation's border buffers?

One primary requirement is the awareness of how an appropriate strategy critically depends on key characteristics of the home economy and society. Nations are highly diverse. Hence, as always, the necessity is different strokes for different folks!

A second primary requirement is to identify workable intermediate positions for the multiple categories of sector-specific transactions. The compromises tailored for each category should well reflect the current and prospective circumstances of both that category and the entire nation. The rationale for those intermediate compromise positions is the same underlying rationale that recommends a middle ground between a Golden Straitjacket (extreme external openness) and a great wall (extreme localist autonomy). The still broader general rationale is the policymakers' needs to, wisely, trade off all the nation's goals against each other. The appropriate policy objective must be to design a suitable overall compromise combination rather than to seek a purist pursuit of only some subset of the goals.

Disagreements about how to manage an open economy frequently stumble over divided views about an appropriate overall stance. The financial aspects in particular are stressful. Policymakers fret over mitigating financial vulnerability to external shock. How much, they ask, can financial border buffers facilitate mitigation?

Some policymakers may be eager to borrow savings from the

rest of the world to promote home growth and development. They may believe, with justification, that the nation has not performed well enough in encouraging and mobilizing the savings of residents. They may argue that economic well-being would fall well short of potential levels if national investments were restricted to the savings that the economy currently generates on its own. With the assistance of foreign investors and creditors, perhaps the nation's enterprises could raise domestic investment well above the flow of national savings. These policymakers' voices suggest that the gross benefits of higher cross-border capital inflows could be substantial. If a nation is smaller or less advanced, such benefits might even be proportionately larger than comparable benefits experienced by financially more advanced nations.

Other policymakers, however, may be wary of financial openness. They may believe, also with justification, that the home financial utilities infrastructure requires strengthening. Without a strong infrastructure, a nation is especially vulnerable to financial instability. Such policymakers welcome a limited amount of foreign direct investment in the economy. But they emphasize that borrowing from abroad can easily be overdone. All policymakers tend to recognize that large amounts of capital inflow may provoke political controversy. Foreign bankers and portfolio investors may be viewed as fickle and inadequately appreciative of the home economy's strengths as well as weaknesses. Possible risks of financial instability may loom large. Under unexpectedly adverse future conditions, it may be feared, the home economy could suffer bad results from financial openness.

The fact that weighty considerations can be advanced on both sides of the debate should drive home policymakers toward a compromise, or intermediate position. A plausible consensus can decide, wisely, to accept some reductions in the nation's de facto autonomy. The benefits resulting from borrowing foreign savings to exploit profitable investment opportunities at home could more than offset the costs from erosion of indigenous values and institutions. A similar outcome could result even from erosion of the ability to sustain local economic conditions that are marginally different from conditions outside the nation. Some protection from external vulnerability is an insurance policy. The plausible compromise is thus to maintain modest frictions between the national financial system and the outside world. That compromise entails crafting financial breakwaters that do not pose dominant obstacles to cross-border financial transactions but still provide modest protection against some of the potential risks and costs.

When designing financial breakwaters, home authorities should proceed especially cautiously if contemplating far-reaching new measures. It is probably easier to get things wrong by erecting new drastic barriers to cross-border transactions than by taking an overly relaxed view. The better choices for a nation over time may depend on the appropriate pace and sequencing for relaxation of existing breakwater measures.

Decisions about financial breakwaters should above all be kept in perspective. In particular, the authorities should pay substantially more attention to their overall monetary and economic policies, and to their prudential oversight and financial standards, than to their breakwater-buffer measures. Breakwater buffers should definitely not be perceived as substitutes for sound national macroeconomic policies, for a suitably chosen exchange regime, for maintenance of a strong international investment position, or for competent supervision and regulation of the financial system generally.

The prudent approach for financial-openness policies has to be pragmatic. It has to be an integrated compromise package reflecting all of the nation's goals. Sound breakwater policies must be context dependent, since no stance will be right for all circumstances and all times. And as the nation's economy and financial system evolve, adjustments and experimentation will be required.

Breakwaters may work better if their main purpose is to moderate unwanted capital inflows rather than stem unwanted capital outflows. If excessive inflows can be moderated in boom times, the nation can better inhibit the emergence of major imbalances and risks. It may be helpful, for example, to adjust the height of a breakwater measure upward when capital inflows are exuberant, especially if foreign investors' perceptions seem increasingly based on short-run herding rather than sound decisions about the medium- and long-run fundamentals of the economy. Prevention of skittish inflows can in turn lower the probability of subsequent outflows in times of disruptive shocks and adversity. An emphasis on inhibiting excessive inflows is more appropriate than waiting to act until a crisis hits, at which time both domestic and foreign residents might be skittishly trying to use the exit option to get funds out of the nation.

Financial breakwater measures intended to be transitory (with a stipulated ending date) might prove more viable than measures intended at the outset to be permanent. Common wisdom in game theory and international relations argues that tying one's hands "permanently" fosters credible commitments. But transitory measures could be more effective than permanent ones because financial breakwaters tend to erode over time. In almost all nations, the financial reservoirs are now more closely connected with the world financial system than was true when communications and information technologies were more limited. New channels for cross-border financial transactions can be devised to evade breakwater measures aimed at existing channels. Governing authorities typically cannot add monitoring and administrative capacities to the supervisory and regulatory agencies as quickly as financial markets can innovate. Wise foresight should caution that it can be increasingly impractical to closely control many types of cross-border capital flows. The policy stances most likely to prevent skittish capital flows seek to avoid the surprises and shocks that give rise to such flows.

Over the longer run, the government's scope for maintaining financial breakwaters could decline further. Progressively more emphasis may have to be placed on managing the risks associated with cross-border finance via general macroprudential and monetary policies rather than by trying to influence them directly via breakwaters. Effective breakwaters can provide greater initial protection for the financial system. Then over time, the breakwaters can be gradually weakened as the financial system becomes more sophisticated and, in particular, as the utilities infrastructure is broadened and strengthened.[8]

## Localist Diversity and a Level Playing Field?

Border buffers inevitably spawn dialogues about equity and fairness across jurisdictions. Controversies about buffers and standards are especially likely when it is alleged that some nations have deliberately created competitive inequities intended to harm the interests of others. Incidents of such international allegations rise as cross-border spillovers increase gradually over time.[9]

Complainers frequently assert that cross-border transactions are unfair if not conducted on a level playing field. Such critics favor, implicitly if not explicitly, the full harmonization of standards across nations, perhaps even the harmonization of governance institutions.

Not surprisingly, protests about a competitively inequitable playing field can be one-sided. Businesses or government officials in "our" nation perceive faulty policies in "other" nations. It is those "foreign" nations that should adjust their policies to moderate or remove the competitive inequities. The level playing field

---

8. For nations at early stages of financial development, breakwaters are likely to play a more prominent role in the development transition than they will play subsequently.

9. For perspective, recall that issues of competitive equity and fairness are prominent even across domestic jurisdictions purely within a single nation.

that my nation wants to play on, in other words, includes the pre-ferred standards already established in my nation.

But cross-national comparisons of competitive equity are subtle. They raise all the deep issues embedded in the over-all trade-off between local autonomy and external openness. Thoughtful compromises lead away from one-sided comparisons of unfair standards in other nations and get transformed into discussions about cross-border cooperation to facilitate resolu-tion of contentious issues.

To be sure, some cross-border differences in policies and standards are not controversial. The speed limits on various seg-ments of home-nation roads, dependent on local conditions and safety requirements, attract no international criticism. The na-tional culture and history taught in home schools is little noticed abroad. If official home documents must use the local language, foreigners typically perceive that requirement as innocuous. Many analogous examples suggest that some localist preferences can flourish without cross-border controversy. Decentralized decisions at the level of the individual nation are deemed satis-factory. Explicit cross-border cooperation with outside nations is deemed unnecessary. Arguments about a level playing field are of little relevance.

Numerous comparative-equity issues, however, are not "local" (national). Many can entail controversy with other na-tions. And because cross-border cooperation may be necessary, decisions cannot be fully decentralized among the relevant indi-vidual nations.

Suppose nation A requires commodities, whether produced at home or abroad, to meet certain design standards to protect the safety of home consumers. Or imagine that nation A prohibits the import of particular medications and food products to protect the safety of home consumers (for example, nonapproved opioid drugs or imports of prepared chicken washed with chlorine). Or consider a requirement that imports of manufactured products into nation

A must be assembled under labor-market working conditions certified to conform to standards approved by home governing authorities. Foreign competitors may find it too expensive to meet such standards. In that event, the standards in nation A act somewhat like tariffs or quotas, effectively diminishing or even eliminating foreign competition for domestic producers.

Suppose nation B relaxes its prudential supervision of financial institutions to foster shallow oversight and reduces its tax rates on their profits to abnormally low levels. The motive for such changes might be a hope to induce foreign financial institutions to relocate some of their activities to nation B. Or imagine that nation C adopts legislation restricting foreign ownership of locally resident facilities for producing goods output and supplying financial services. The underlying motive in that case might be to reduce foreign activity in nation C's home economy.

For a still more complex case, assume that the governing authorities of nation D believe the nation is too poor to afford the costs of a squeaky-clean environment and they therefore maintain regulations that permit some production of goods that significantly pollute local air and water supplies. Suppose nations E and F, in contrast, impose tight restrictions on emissions of pollutants. Nation D may then argue that it is inappropriate for other nations like E and F to impute to nation D the value they themselves place on a clean environment—just as it would be inappropriate to impute nation D's valuations to the local environments of nations E and F.

Comparisons such as these are the proximate sparks for complaints that cross-border business is not conducted on a level playing field. Again, the typical complaint from abroad about individual home nations A, B, C, and D is that those home nations inappropriately demand that the correct leveled playing field is the one established already within their own borders.

Arguments for creation of a level playing field for a substantive area of national standards entail advocating the harmonization across nations of those standards. Commentators espousing the merits of a leveled playing field seldom acknowledge this point.

The mantra of a level playing field for the world economy is troublesome. It is frequently misused as a facile argument for unfettered cross-border transactions. Remember that the Golden Straitjacket approach downplays the preservation of valued features of local autonomy. That approach is particularly unpersuasive if advocates of unfettered external openness go so far as to call for a leveled playing field across all nation-states and for virtually every substantive issue.

International trade occurs precisely because of differences among nations—in resource endowments, labor skills, and consumer tastes. Nations specialize in producing goods and services in which they are, relatively, most efficient. In a fundamental sense, cross-border transactions are valuable precisely because the playing field is not level (chapter 2). British economist David Ricardo (1772–1823), who long ago initially developed the theory of comparative advantage, focused on differences among nations due to resources or technology. But Ricardo could also have ascribed the productive differences to differing national environmental standards or social climates as well as to physical or technological resources. Taking all "climatic" differences as a given, the theory of comparative advantage argues that free trade among nations tends to enhance global well-being.

Taken to its logical extreme, the cliché of leveling the playing field implies that nations should converge so as eventually to become nearly homogeneous. Yet the recommendation for homogenization—for sweeping harmonization—is unrealistic and, for some parts of life, even pernicious. The case for an anticosmopolitan, anti-level-playing-field position is consistent with own-nation localism and buffer-fence zones that inhibit losses of effective autonomy.

A core argument supporting localist leanings in the direction of national autonomy is that a home nation's residents should be permitted to arrange their lives and resources in accord with their own preferences. When that perspective is emphasized, the notion of a level playing field appears to be an unhelpful mantra. It is a rule of thumb that can mislead even though it apparently advances the plausible-sounding objective of competitive equity across nations.

## International Minimum Standards for All Jurisdictions?

The fantasy that all policies for all nations should be harmonized therefore deserves dismissal. Yet it is essential to acknowledge that some border buffers for individual nations can be harmful to others. Truly objectionable national policies deserve to be criticized and revised.

For example, what if nation K's negligent product standards for medications and prepared foods imported into nation A do really endanger the safety of nation A's consumers? What if nation K's manufactured goods exported to nation A are in fact assembled under labor-market conditions much less supportive of workers' rights than products made by nation A firms? For those firms and other nation A residents, K's policies will be perceived as unsafe, unfair, and competitively inequitable.

Nation B's prudential supervision of its financial institutions, if carelessly lax, can justifiably attract criticism that B is, in part, unfairly trying to induce foreign financial institutions to relocate business in nation B. Or if nation C's regulations restricting foreign ownership of locally resident banks really are unduly harsh, foreigners can understandably claim that they are inappropriately being denied access to conduct business in nation C.

Which perspective about differences across nations is more compelling? Are nation K's standards and regulations resembling protectionist measures merely exercising K's national preferences, appropriately exploiting its comparative advantage in goods that are less safe to produce and made under labor-market working conditions traditional in nation K? Or are K's standards and regulations in fact intended to diminish or eliminate foreign competition for domestic producers in other nations?

Could nation B just be highlighting its natural advantages as a financial center—or is that nation unfairly subsidizing foreign banks to relocate? Are nation C's restrictions on foreign ownership merely preserving a local preference for home institutions to be locally owned—or are the restrictions pointedly aimed at reducing foreign activity in nation C's economy?

Questions of this nature can only be addressed area by area, by examining in detail, carefully and dispassionately, the cross-nation comparisons. Yet cross-nation analysis and negotiations about such difficult issues are highly problematic.

Because numerous areas exist where cross-national differences in border buffers are contentious, a further question naturally arises. For difficult cases, shouldn't cross-border cooperation lead to agreement on some *minimum standards* to be adhered to by all nations?

The issue of international cooperation for minimum standards is highlighted by the subset of nations referred to as offshore financial centers (OFCs). The banks and other financial institutions in OFCs foster regulatory arbitrage and supervisory laxity as a way of promoting their attractiveness as locations for financial activity.[10]

---

10. Locations referred to as OFCs in the Caribbean area include Anguilla, Antigua and Barbuda, Aruba, Belize, the British Virgin Islands, the Cayman Islands, Costa Rica, the Bahamas, Barbados, Bermuda, the Netherlands Antilles, Panama, St. Kitts and Nevis, St. Lucia, St. Vincent and the Grenadines, and Turks and Caicos. Those located in the Middle East include Bahrain, Lebanon, and the United Arab Emirates. OFCs located in Asia and Oceania include Singapore, Hong Kong, the Philippines, Macau, Labuan (Malaysia), Mauritius, the

Overall, OFCs are heterogeneous. Some have relatively well-supervised financial institutions. They acknowledge that a cooperative strengthening of the infrastructures for national financial systems is a global public good. Such OFCs act responsibly to cooperate with international initiatives to improve financial standards and to strengthen national financial infrastructures.

Many OFCs, however, seem content with weak financial standards and prudential oversight. Many intentionally restrict transparency in disclosure policies. Many display a limited willingness to cooperate internationally. From the perspective of the world community of nations, it seems justified to label those OFCs renegade jurisdictions. The need to judge which jurisdictions are acting irresponsibly and failing to cooperate with collective efforts to enhance stability of the world financial system is an example of the broader need for improved international monitoring and assessment of financial systems.

To the degree that renegade jurisdictions abet financial crime and money laundering, fail to discourage financial transactions associated with terrorist groups, maintain little or no taxation of capital themselves, or do not discourage tax evasion or improper tax avoidance, the governing authorities of responsible nations have additional valid arguments for maintaining some regulations and restraints on private financial transactions, and for considering certain breakwater measures to inhibit cross-border transactions. Such crime-prevention and tax-compliance motives in those nations may not stem from a wish to discriminate in favor of domestic residents over foreign residents. Rather, if responsible nations

---

Seychelles, Guam, Vanuatu (New Hebrides), Samoa, the Cook Islands, the Marshall Islands, Nauru, and Niue Island. OFCs in Europe include Luxembourg, Andorra, Liechtenstein, Cyprus, the Channel Islands (Jersey and Guernsey), the Isle of Man, Malta, Gibraltar, and Monaco. For an overview as of 2011, see Philip R. Lane and Gian Maria Milesi-Ferretti, "Cross-Border Investment in Small International Financial Centers" (IMF, 2011). Also Bertaut, Bressler, and Curcuru, "Globalization and the Geography of Capital Flows" (2018).

decide to respond with prudential restraints or breakwater measures, the dominant motive could be to prevent illegal or damaging activity by either domestic or foreign residents.

Terrorism, financial crime, and money laundering are reminders that reprehensible elements exist in financial systems. An individual nation may not be an offshore financial center, nor be accused of laxity in its prudential oversight or its regulations inhibiting money laundering and tax evasion. But no nation is impervious to criminal activities. Not even the most ardent proponents of unfettered capital flows would apply the "freedom" argument to assets and liabilities incurred through criminal activities.

If a small financial-center nation has lax standards—lower than those in other nations—only for the purpose of attracting financial activities within its borders, why should other nations agree to let those lax standards continue? The regulatory forbearance of the offending jurisdiction certainly harms other jurisdictions. It produces gains for that location precisely because it harms others.

Responsible regulatory standards and prudential oversight cannot be magic bullets that inhibit all financial difficulties. Even with further improvements in nations' regulations and oversight, financial problems now and again are sure to arise. Individual nations, most of all offshore financial centers, should strengthen standards and oversight over time.

Vigor and stability of financial and economic activity in the wider world community depend to some degree on a universal presence of sound financial standards and effective prudential oversight. Weakness in a few spots can cause widespread contagion and damage elsewhere. Support for strong financial stability throughout the world thus leads inevitably to demands for collective action for the design and implementation of minimum international standards. The minimum standards should ideally apply everywhere, to all nations.

To repeat, the simple notion that a leveled playing field should uniformly apply to standards and border buffers for all functional areas, including financial, should be set aside. Some degree of localist emphasis, nation by nation, is desirable. Hence some degree of diversity across nations is desirable, too. But a strong case also exists, in the area of financial supervision especially, for minimum international standards adhered to by a large majority of (and preferably all) nations.

A recommendation espousing minimum international standards for the regulation and prudential oversight of financial institutions applies to many other functional areas of economic and social activity. Indeed, my conjecture is that when analysts in the second half of the twenty-first century look in the rear-view mirror, they will identify numerous instances where the now-current tensions and complaints about unlevel playing fields will have fostered the widespread adoption of minimum international standards.

The mantra for leveling the playing field implies, again, that nations should converge so as to eventually become nearly homogeneous. But that recommendation is too often made without grappling with considerations that cut in the contrary direction. Yet antipathy to a level playing field should not be taken to an extreme either. Minimum standards are often helpful and sometimes necessary.

The appropriate mantra for many functional areas is to favor a middle way between the extremes: a playing field for cross-border interactions that allows for differences across nations but at the same time often endorses common minimum global standards.[11]

---

11. International discussions among national governments and their regulatory agencies have tended to move in this direction. In a variety of substantive areas, actual agreements—often with extensive details—already exist.

Out of the crooked timber of humanity,
no straight thing was ever made.

*Immanuel Kant,* Idea for a General History with a
Cosmopolitan Purpose *(1784), Proposition 6*

# 5. Cross-Border Migration of People

The discussion now turns to border buffers for influencing the movements of people in and out of nations. No other subject in the book is more fraught and difficult.

Here I emphasize the perspective of an individual nation receiving immigrants. A fuller overview would also discuss procedures and regulations of transit localities and of the sending nations from which emigration occurs. Substantial scope exists for both friction and cooperation among recipient, transit, and sending nations.[1]

Box 5-1 organizes the issues related to border buffers and the cross-migration of people into separate topics. For instance, policymakers in a recipient home nation require monitoring,

---

1. The demands of this book for brevity and for an eagle's-flight perspective cause it to fall far short of a comprehensive overview of cross-border migration issues. For a helpful ambitious overview, see Paul Collier, *Exodus: Immigration and Multiculturalism in the 21st Century* (2014). For another overview, see Helliwell, Layard, and Sachs, *World Happiness Report* (2018, chapter 1, "Happiness and Migration: An Overview"). A large literature of course exists for historical episodes of migration (dating back centuries).

information gathering, and analytical oversight of cross-border movements. Governance oversight and administrative implementation need to be backstopped by several local institutions. Immigration is classified into three categories: first, people seeking refugee-asylum status; second, people legally seeking status as economic migrants (not refugee-asylum status); and finally, people attempting to enter the nation illegally.

This chapter and box 5-1 emphasize several distinctions regarding cross-border movements. For example, there are differences between legal and illegal immigration and how the two groups are treated. There are also differences among types of cross-border movements of people according to whether immigrants intend to be permanent, persisting for a long period, or temporary (in and out for shorter periods).

The most critical differentiation is between refugee-asylum seekers and people who are motivated as economic migrants. This distinction has pervasive significance both legally and substantively. Refugees and asylum seekers are trying to escape political persecution or violence in their own countries. Alternatively, they may have experienced severe natural disasters and hope to be successful applicants on humanitarian grounds. In contrast, economic migrants hope to succeed as immigrants because they aspire to leave behind poor living conditions. They want to improve their economic status in a more prosperous environment. Economic migrants do not leave their nation of origin primarily because of persecution or natural disaster. Economic migrants do not qualify under the legal criteria for refugee status and are not legally entitled to receive international protections accorded to refugees.

The distinction is central even though it can be murky to implement in practice. When assessing their own status, individual applicants have incentives to embellish or falsify. Some applicants for refugee or asylum status, for example, may greatly exaggerate the degree to which they have been persecuted or subjected to natural disasters. Individuals or families who are predominantly motivated as economic migrants may falsely use the entry channel of genuine refugee-asylum seekers, thereby trying to buttress their hopes for acceptance. Immigration officials in the nation where entry is sought often cannot make reliable judgments to separate economic migrants from refugees and asylum seekers.

The logic of distinguishing refugees from other migrants dates back to the aftermath of World War II. The distinction was embedded in the United Nations Convention and Protocol Relating to the Status of Refugees (1951) and was carried forward in the 1967 Protocol Relating to the Status of Refugees.

The separation has always been questioned. As the journalist Masha Gessen has asked, for example:

> [What is] a meaningful way to distinguish between economic and political disenfranchisement? What about a well-founded fear of violence and death? Does a seriously ill girl from Honduras deserve to die more than does a gay man who could be executed in Iran? Does a taxi-driver from Brazil deserve to risk violence at the hands of a gang more than a Russian journalist deserves to risk it at the hands of the government? Does a woman deserve to face rape and beatings at the hands of her husband more than a Syrian man deserves to be executed by ISIS? These questions are impossible to answer, and the comparisons, of course, are absurd.[2]

Terminology itself is problematic. *Refugee, asylum,* and *economic migrant* are used confusingly. For legal clarity and conformity with international agreements, *refugee* and *migrant* should not be combined. If striving for clarity, journalists and pundits should reserve the label *refugee* for cases where persecution or disaster experience is unambiguous. The phrase *economic refugee* should not be used to refer to an economic migrant.

2. Masha Gessen (June 2018).

Box 5-1. **Classification of Issues about Border Buffers for Cross-Border Migration of People into Recipient Nations**

1. **Monitoring, Information-Gathering, and Analytical Oversight**
   - Collection of data on current and past cross-border migration flows
   - Forward-looking procedures and institutions to adapt to changed circumstances

2. **Governance Oversight and Administrative Implementation of Policies, Regulations, and Procedures**
   - Institutions predominantly involved vary from nation to nation
   - Different institutions and administration for asylum and nonasylum cases

3. **Immigration into Home Nation of Legal Applicants Seeking Asylum/Refugee Status**

   3a. **Targets, Procedures, and Regulations for Asylum Applicants**
   - Differential treatments for asylum/refugee cases
     - Adults
     - Children and families

   3b. **Criteria and Political Loci for Policy Decisions about Permitted Asylum Immigration**

   3c. **Criteria and Political Loci for Return of Refugees to Nations of Origin after Abatement of Persecution and Natural-Disaster Conditions in Nations of Origin**

4. **Immigration into Home Nation of Legal Applicants Seeking Nonasylum Status**

   4a. **Targets and Procedures for Legal Nonasylum Migrants**
   - Criteria for temporary, persisting, or permanent immigration
   - Criteria for policy decisions about permitted levels
     - Adults
     - Children and families

- Criteria for prioritizing different nonasylum groups for potential approval of entry
  - Skills with local language(s)
  - Merit selection by work skills/experience and education
    - Visas for prearranged employment offers from local employers
  - Differential treatment of families and ages
    - Nuclear versus extended families
  - Other considerations that potentially facilitate local assimilation
  - Provisional visas—Registered Provisional Immigrants (RPIs) versus Legal Permanent Residents (LPRs) versus applicants for naturalization and citizenship

### 4b. Regulations and Continuing Provisions for Nonasylum Migrants

- Temporary
- Longer-run and potential permanent residents

### 4c. Requirements and Procedures for Naturalization and Eventual Citizenship

## 5. Policies and Procedures for Border Control and Illegal Immigration

### 5a. Civil Law and Criminal Law Aspects

### 5b. Resources Allocated to Border Control and Monitoring

### 5c. Procedures for Managing Deportations and for Illegal Immigrants in Custody

- Adults
- Children and families

### 5d. Eventual Legalization of Illegal Immigrants

For strict accuracy, one should differentiate refugees from asylum seekers. A refugee is a person who has fled his or her place of origin and is unable or unwilling to return because of natural disaster or "a well-founded fear of being persecuted for their race, religion, nationality, or membership of a particular social group or political opinion."[3] Authorities in the nation where entry is sought or in an international entity such as the United Nations Refugee Agency determine whether a person seeking international protection meets the criteria. An asylum seeker is an individual who searches for international protection and whose claim has not yet been finally resolved by the nation to which he or she has applied. Not every asylum seeker will ultimately be recognized as a refugee, but every refugee is initially an asylum seeker.

Analysis of the pros and cons of all types of immigration stumbles on hard questions of whether the immigration is judged to be beneficial or adverse, and to which parties. Whose perceptions should receive the greater weight in judging? A migrant person or family have presumably acted on a judgment that their migration would sooner or later benefit them. Net effects on people left behind in the nation of origin are uncertain. The most contentious issues are whether the net effects on the indigenous population in the recipient nation will be judged locally as beneficial, and how the gross and net effects are distributed among individual residents and groups. Judgments depend on a convoluted nexus of concerns: moral, humanitarian, security, social, economic, and political.

A handful of cases may be perceived as beneficial because the interests of the immigrants and indigenous home residents broadly coincide. If the supply of particular types of home labor

3. UNHCR (United Nations High Commission for Refugees), *Convention and Protocol Relating to the Status of Refugees* (2010), p. 3.

falls short of demand, an inflow of immigrant labor with those skills may be generally welcome. If there is a new product not yet made at home and if new foreign-owned production facilities employing immigrant workers can be established to make the product domestically without displacing existing local production and jobs, the net effects can be perceived by almost all concerned as beneficial.

Temporary workers are another example where the benefits can be mutual. Short-term inflows of foreign workers to harvest agricultural crops can help local residents earn income from production while providing temporary employment for foreign labor. This will be welcome if little concern exists about displacement of jobs for local workers. Specific illustrations include temporary seasonal movements of agricultural laborers into the United Kingdom from Romania and Bulgaria or of fruit and vegetable pickers into California from Mexico and other Latin American countries.

The most beneficial cases are those where both local residents and foreign immigrants experience net gains, and where the gross costs to individual local residents are small (and hence do not raise the awkward issue of redistribution and compensation to adversely affected local residents). I conjecture that the majority of historical cases of immigration involved large net gains for the migrants and small net gains for most of the indigenous recipient populations.

Nonetheless, judgments about the net effects of the majority of immigration flows tend to be contentious within recipient nations. Individual local residents and groups are likely to experience dislocation and adverse consequences. That is true whether the migrants are permanent, persisting, or temporary. Influxes of immigrants, even if the recipient nation as a whole enjoys net total gains, can be controversial. For instance, plumbers in France and the United Kingdom assert that Polish plumbers are taking away their indigenous clientele. As with the benefits of ex-

ternal openness more generally, the distribution of net gains—
along with the issue of whether and how to compensate those
who incur net losses—rises insistently to the surface of private
and official debates.

*Illegal immigration*—entry to a recipient nation without con-
forming to its procedures and laws—obviously raises numerous
additional issues. Analysis of these is even more fraught and difficult than those mentioned already. Each of the following questions is important.

- Should illegal immigration be treated as an infringement of
  civil law or as a violation of criminal law? Alternative answers to this question have quite different implications for
  how home enforcement authorities, home courts, and home
  judges handle illegal immigration.

- Should recipient-nation officials try to distinguish between
  people apprehended for illegal entry according to whether
  they may or may not have a potential claim to be classified
  as a refugee?

- How much emphasis should be given to home-nation laws
  relative to existing international norms and agreements
  (which typically do not have enforcement mechanisms—see
  further discussion below)?

- What agreements and cooperative measures may be feasible
  between a recipient nation and the governing authorities of
  the nation of origin or of nations that illegal immigrants
  pass through prior to detention?

- What are appropriate penalties and punishments for at-
  tempted illegal immigration? How do such penalties and
  punishments affect the incentives for illegal immigration?
  Are there other effective ways to discourage incentives of
  migrants who try to enter illegally?

- Should home monitoring and enforcement against illegal immigration be separate from policing and enforcement of infractions of domestic procedures and laws? Should a nation's official military organizations be involved in monitoring and enforcement of illegal immigration? What civil laws and criminal laws should authorize, and constrain, home enforcement? Are special enforcement difficulties encountered, and different procedures needed, with family units that include children?

Straightforward agreed answers to these questions are not readily available, even to lawyers and officials with expertise.

The questions about illegal immigration presage further questions about the monitoring and vetting procedures that apply to applications for immigration. Monitoring and vetting is typically different, and should be different, at stages beyond initial entry. Procedures presumably also should be different for legal versus illegal immigrants. Whatever choices are made to implement the murky distinction between refugees and economic migrants are necessarily dependent on the skills and experiences of vetting officials. Special services and knowledge are required to process family units with children. Special expertise is required for evaluating fraudulent paperwork and for judging the situations of people apprehended for illegal entry.

A nation's policymakers, both internally and through their contacts with policymakers abroad, should emphasize clarity, transparency, and consistency over time. If standards, regulations, and criteria embedded in their separation fences (see chapters 2 and 4) for managing migration flows do not have those characteristics, the measures will not be well understood nor adequately observed. They then will have little possibility of encouraging the desired incentives and individual behaviors essential for the migration laws and procedures to work smoothly. Clarity, transparency, and consistency over time are indispensable for a sensible system, either for a single nation, an allied group of nations, or the world as a whole.

Detailed plans for separation fences for the cross-border movements of people must be context dependent, varying nation by nation. Differentiation between refugees and economic migrants must also be context dependent. The specifics are invariably decisive. The inherent moral and humanitarian dilemmas and the complex "insider-us" versus "outsider-them" tensions can seldom be deliberated without anguish.

Given the difficulties, the remaining observations here tackle the cross-border migration of people from even more of an eagle's-flight perspective.

Should the borders of a nation be monitored and controlled? A first response to this question might be suspicion. The query seems poorly formulated, implying overly simple alternative choices. A second response might be unambiguous to the overly simple question: Yes, definitely! Completely free migration into and out of nations is impossible for practical political reasons. Such uninhibited migration would be inconsistent with even moderate insider attitudes. Nations need separation fences to monitor and control cross-border movements. That need is especially significant for nations that are more prosperous and hence most sought as targets for entry.

To repeat, true refugees cannot invariably be differentiated from would-be economic migrants. And yes, venomous nationalist arguments for keeping out "inferior" foreigners often fly surreptitiously under the radar. But no rich nation can realistically accept an unlimited obligation to welcome throngs of economic migrants from poorer nations. It is a pipedream to imagine unfettered openness and the welcoming of unregulated migration.

The point can be taken even further. It is a disservice to frame the general debate as between supporters of open borders and supporters of enforcing immigration laws. Both the existence of borders and the need and right to police them tend to be unquestioned assumptions in the beliefs of practical people. Completely unfettered movements of people across borders is an impractical idea for virtually all nations. Humanitarian generosity is consonant with prudent enforcement of controls on migration. It is not necessary to downplay inward-looking national identity to avoid the evils of populist nationalism.

Again, neither the extremes of xenophobia nor xenophilia are practical. James Traub aptly criticizes xenophilia:

> For mobile, prosperous, worldly people, the cherishing of diversity is a cardinal virtue; we dote on difference. That's simply not true for many people who can't choose where to live, or who prefer the familiar coordinates of their life. That was the bitter lesson that British cosmopolites learned from Brexit. If the answer is to insist that the arrival of vast numbers of new people on our doorstep is an unmixed blessing, and that those who believe otherwise are Neanderthals, then we leave the field wide open to Donald J. Trump and Geert Wilders and Marine Le Pen.[4]

A sensible approach avoids the polar extremes and finds an "in-betweener" middle ground. Paul Collier's thoughtful book rests in that middle ground.[5] Jeffrey Sachs, in an interview in 2017, firmly occupies that ground:[6]

> If people [residents of poorer nations] were told that they could move [freely across borders], no questions asked, probably a billion would shift around the planet within five years, with many coming to Europe or the U.S. No society would tolerate even a fraction of that flow. Any politician who says, "Let's be generous," without saying "We're not going to throw the doors wide open,"

4. Traub (March 7, 2017).

5. Collier (2014).

6. The interview by Jeffrey Sachs was published in *Project Syndicate* (February 3, 2017).

will lose. So, I think that's where the left is tongue-tied, because it sounds chauvinistic to say we need a limit on migration. . . .

Yes, borders can and should be policed. Of course, refugees fleeing for their lives must be helped. That's not only basic human decency; it's also international law. But refugees and economic migrants are two different matters. No rich country is under the obligation to open its doors to all of the economic migrants that would come. . . .

The left doesn't have a language that acknowledges the need for borders and the need to police them. I'm not in favor of a wall, per se, but I am in favor of regulated borders, not an open door to unregulated migration. All high-income countries need borders. Borders do not mean closed doors or bans (like Trump's), least of all religiously based bans, which are deeply offensive and self-defeating. But borders do mean enforcement of limits to migration. . . .

We need borders. And we should police them. We should have migration, because diversity is good; but we should not have open doors, because we can't afford it, and we don't want it. I think the most basic idea that needs to be worked out is managed migration, whereby people arrive legally at a certain rate that is proportionate to the country's size and pace of demographic change. . . .

The first distinction is refugees and non-refugees. We have international law on refugees, based on the principle of non-refoulement: you can't return refugees to a place where they are likely to be persecuted. A refugee is someone who is fleeing persecution, and the first thing you want to do to resolve a refugee crisis is to stop the underlying cause.

A middle-ground stance sensitive to humanitarian concerns might insist even more than the Sachs interview on preserving the legal and practical separation between refugees and nonrefugees. The conviction that monitoring and policing of a nation's borders is warranted must not undermine the humanitarian conviction that asylum seekers and refugees have rights of access when fleeing from persecution and natural disasters. The existing international norms and procedures for refugees and asylum seekers say that if a person gets inside the border of a nation other than their own, they have a protected right to request asylum. The entered nation is obligated to hear and evaluate the claim. It cannot expel the asylum seeker while processing the claim or if the seeker faces a credible threat from persecution within their nation of origin. If the entered nation finds the seeker meets the criteria for a refugee, it is obligated to provide shelter. If the seeker does not meet the criteria, only then can the seeker be expelled.

Refugees' rights became enshrined in international law through the global agreements in 1951 and 1967. Not all nations signed the agreements, but they and their norms are understood to be widely accepted. To some degree they constrain all nations. The norms were a result of the large numbers of refugees created in Europe in the wake of World War II. The end of colonialism further increased refugees. The war's victors spent much of the next decade establishing a revised international order with associated national laws.

The postwar international agreements did not contain enforcement mechanisms. Therefore, essentially nothing prevented a nation from repealing its refugee and asylum laws or, if the home government could get away with it, ignoring them. Thanks to a loophole in international procedures dating from the 1990s, it now seems widely accepted that a nation can avoid its humanitarian responsibilities to refugees by forcibly preventing them from reaching its borders. Violations of the spirit and even the laws of the international agreements became more common in the final decades of the twentieth century and in the initial years of the twenty-first century.[7]

Sadly, the global dimensions of refugee arrangements have become more and more stressed. More advanced nations con-

---

7. My generalizations rely on a survey article by Max Fisher and Amanda Taub in the *New York Times* (November 2–3, 2018). The quotation from them is from the article.

tinue to pretend that they support rights and protections. But simultaneously these nations shift the burdens onto poorer nations that are less likely or able to protect refugees. Because they know that advanced nations will look the other way, the poorer nations do not feel compelled to provide full protections. The poorer nations may prevent refugees from working or restrict where they can live. They may sometimes force refugees to return home before it is safe for them to do so.

"What we have now," Max Fisher and Amanda Taub conclude, "isn't a global refugee system so much as a loose network of occasionally and partially observed norms. This means that there is no reliable process for relieving the political, social and economic pressures that sudden refugee influxes create. This creates dangers primarily for refugees but also for the governments that have deconstructed the system."[8]

Populist and nationalist politics also adversely influence the refugee and asylum issues. Excessive localist politics within recipient nations, skeptical of international agreements and immigration, have little interest in asylum's basic concepts of universal rights and global burden-sharing. It takes a long time to build international norms. In recent years it has seemed easier to dismantle them. If the dismantling is not reversed, millions of people displaced by war or persecution may have to go without the protections once promised by a world that had agreed "Never again."

How can remedial actions be taken to dampen the incentives for surges of cross-border migration? The beginning of wisdom about this question is to understand the underlying causes of refugee and economic-migrant crises. The most promising types of mitigating actions require that the spotlight be shined on sending nations. What can be done there to reduce the pressures for outgoing migration? Ideally, cooperation between both sending

8. Ibid.

and recipient nations would foster the design and implementation of actions.

The fundamental point for regions and the planet as a whole is that enhancing development and well-being in poorer regions, thereby reducing incentives to leave, is preferred to facilitating migration from poorer regions to economically more advanced ones. This point applies to economic migrants even more than those who quality as refugees and asylum seekers, but it does apply to both.

Most residents of more advanced regions will prefer that strategy. Many residents of poorer nations will also likely share that view. If all types of costs are taken into account, such strategies may be significantly less costly over a longer run. They have the potential to mitigate tensions and avert conflicts that turn to violence.

Development assistance from advanced nations to developing nations comes with notable headaches and weaknesses of its own. Political consensus for such assistance to mitigate migration crises is weak, and sometimes absent altogether.

Yet support for development within sending regions can bolster governing authorities when they are willing to ameliorate domestic persecution, violence, and crime. If local political malfeasance or domestic corruption in sending regions is contributing to a migration crisis, pressure from governments in recipient nations may help to redress the problems. Development assistance from abroad can contribute to recovery and longer-run recuperation from natural disasters.

Reducing the pressures for outgoing migration from sending nations is far from easy. Yet the fundamental point is powerful: Fostering development in poorer nations is a much better remedy for discouraging outward migration to economically more advanced regions.

Over the longer run, improvements will be needed in the international norms and broad agreements. The short-run prospects are discouraging. The lamentable state of international laws and agreements for refugees and asylum seekers is likewise manifest more generally in international norms and agreements covering economic migrants. Eventually, a humane world requires forward progress supported by enhanced international comity.

To remind yourself of what can go wrong and the urgent needs for improvement, simply recollect the twenty-first century refugee and migrant crises in Syria, Iraq, Turkey, Jordan, Yemen, Myanmar, Indonesia, Australia, southern Europe, Central America, Mexico, and the southern border of the United States.

A thoughtful reader of an earlier draft found my observations about migration "a bit too negative." But I do not tilt toward a negative view. The benefits of migration and labor mobility are one of the great positive features of external openness. The potential benefits are prodigious for migrants themselves. More can and should be said about the potential benefits of migration for recipient nations (especially those with supportive social policies). Like my critical reader, I worry that recent frictions about cross-border flows of people have permitted migration to become a scapegoat for other policy failures in recipient nations (such as lack of adequate housing and lack of adequate health insurance).

A concluding thought: In the shorter run, every nation should implement a responsible set of policies for cross-border migration. The details, as always, must differ across nations and be context dependent. What qualifies as "responsible" will invariably be contentious. But it is surely a minimum obligation to the world community to have explicit policies and make them clear and transparent.

# 6. External Imbalances and Exchange Rates

## Imbalances in Cross-Border Interactions

The interactions of a nation across its borders are the result of a multitude of decentralized decisions by residents and outsider foreigners. Just as with interactions among domestic residents, the decentralized decisions are not normally a focus of governance. Cross-border interactions, however, can at times become unbalanced in the aggregate. They then become problematic. Imbalances can generate friction and controversy. At that point they require national policy attention.

Some external imbalances are not worrisome. Indeed, some are collectively helpful. Furthermore, some imbalances—even if deemed unwanted—eventually can be sustained for long periods. The dilemma is that some external imbalances are unwelcome and unsustainable. Those imbalances inevitably require adjustment, sooner or later. If they are not adjusted, harmful consequences may accumulate and eventually force painful and still more adverse adjustments.

An example of a helpful aggregate imbalance—one persisting

for a long period and not requiring adjustment—is when a nation experiences a continuing excess of imports over exports of goods and services associated with a boom in national investment. In such cases, foreign owners of capital participating in the local boom cover the deficit in goods and services trade.

A second example of a helpful imbalance may occur when a nation has a continuing influx of immigrants wishing to participate in the national economy by supplying labor for expanding local economic activity. That imbalance can be deemed helpful provided that local citizens welcome the additional labor supplied by foreigners. If an upsurge in immigration is not welcomed by local citizens, of course the imbalance would be deemed problematic and trigger political opposition.

An unsustainable imbalance occurs if, for example, overly exuberant local demand for foreign-produced goods generates persistent current-account deficits. When such unwanted deficits cannot be sustained by net inflows of private capital, they eventually must be adjusted. If concern mounts high enough, net private capital flows may turn to outflows rather than inflows, thereby generating greater pressure for adjustment. If a nation runs persistent surpluses on its current account, less pressure may exist for adjustment in the shorter run, especially locally at home. Even then, however, eventual adjustment is likely.

"Official settlements" deficits or surpluses can be especially problematic. (Aggregate imbalances in official settlements refer to the net sum of all balance-of-payments transactions except current-account transactions and all private capital flows.) A highly unwelcome official-settlements deficit occurs if, for example, a nation simultaneously experiences a persisting current-account deficit and a persisting deficit in the net private capital account, thereby causing a persisting downward trend in the nation's official reserve assets.

Policy responses can be sluggish and deferred. But adjustment of some external imbalances cannot be deferred forever.

Potential adjustment mechanisms need to be available. Balance-of-payments crises, should they occur, virtually force national authorities to respond with policy changes.

Policy actions to foster adjustments to unsustainable external imbalances are headaches that can arise for the governing authorities of any nation. Those imbalances influence key aspects of the nation's economy, polity, and social systems. Understanding and coping with how unwelcome imbalances in cross-border relationships are adjusted is at the core of how nations cope with the trade-offs between local autonomy and external openness.

## Trade-off Choices for a Nation's Financial Governance

National decisionmakers espouse numerous goals. They are expected to support all facets of home life: political, economic and financial, cultural, social, religious and secular.

Given the dissimilarities among nations, larger nations act differently from smaller, richer from poorer, advanced from developing. Nations with financial centers—such as London in the United Kingdom, New York in the United States, Tokyo in Japan, Singapore and Hong Kong and Bahrain—experience different financial problems from nations that are less specialized in finance.

Available policy instruments vary from nation to nation. The variety of instruments capable of influencing cross-border interactions was identified earlier (chapters 4 and 5). Dissimilarities are pronounced in the utilities infrastructures supporting national economic and financial systems. The conduct of macroeconomic policies is especially diverse across nations.

Macroeconomic policies critically influence the general climate within which a nation's financial system and the wider economy operate. Both the monetary policies of a nation's central bank and the fiscal policies of home governance institutions—budget revenues and expenditures, and the balance among them—are critical components of the general macroeconomic environment. Financial stability depends on sound supervisory and regulatory oversight. A wise use of macroeconomic and prudential-oversight instruments is no less a public good, and no less vital, than many other collective goods supplied by government.

The following list of goals is a reminder of how the manner and degree of external openness influences virtually all aspects of the home nation's economy, policy, and society. Home policy-makers seek:

- avoidance of sharp fluctuations in output and employment (no recessionary busts or excessive booms);

- maintenance of reasonable price stability (no pronounced, persistent inflation or deflation in the prices of goods and services);

- continued robust growth and development of the economy;

- rapid adoption of technological innovations and new products originating abroad that can be favorable for raising home productivity and incomes;

- preservation of a stable, smoothly operating, and efficient home financial reservoir;

- maintenance of accounting and audit procedures, financial standards, and legal processes and institutions to underpin the economy and financial system;

- collective leadership in the event of financial crises ("lender-of-last-resort" function of providing emergency assistance to temporarily illiquid and troubled financial institutions);

- reduction of poverty within the nation, and encouragement of less inequality in the distribution of income and wealth;

- monitoring of the nation's external vulnerability, and, to the extent feasible, shoring up of the nation's ability to adjust to adverse developments (originating either at home or abroad);

- avoidance of disruptive fluctuations in the nation's exchange rate and unsustainable trends in the nation's balance-of-payments and international investment positions; and

- establishment of a reputation for the nation as a responsible component of the regional and world economy (no perceptions by the rest of the world that the nation is a renegade jurisdiction).

Exchange-rate arrangements are at the center of a nation's policy nexus. They influence virtually all its goals.

Many larger nations have their own separate currency unit. The central bank is then responsible for managing institutions and procedures that help to determine rates of exchange with foreign currencies. Other nations do not have their own separate currencies. And some nations choose to belong to a currency union where all the member nations share a common currency.

For nations that maintain their own separate currency, national economic and financial life is markedly different from that of nations that do not maintain their own currency. Private views about currencies, exchange rates, and exchange arrangements, and even public-sector views, are often overly simple and ill-advised. Many pundits in business circles and the news media regard the choice of exchange regime as the most important decision to be made by a nation's government. Some go still further to presume that other national choices pale in significance provided that the choice of exchange regime is made correctly.

Any exchange regime is afflicted by uncertainties. Any exchange regime will reflect and exacerbate financial turbulence if a nation adopts seriously faulty macroeconomic policies and inadequate prudential-oversight policies. No exchange regime can insulate the nation from unexpected adverse shocks, originating either at home or abroad. When national policies are unsound or when adverse shocks are large, the financial system can readily fall into trouble. The world capital markets can lose confidence in the nation, which can then suffer large disruptions—no matter what the exchange regime may be.

One of the easiest ways for a nation to get into financial trouble is to peg its exchange rate when evolving circumstances could benefit from adjustments in the rate. Yet a floating exchange rate will not prevent trouble if domestic policies are badly out of whack or if foreign financial markets lose confidence.

The more open a nation's financial system is to the rest of the world and the fewer its buffers inhibiting cross-border transactions, the greater its vulnerability to unexpected adverse shocks and unsound home policies. Complete freedom for cross-border financial transactions can certainly undermine any regime that pegs exchange rates to foreign currencies. Yet complete freedom can also facilitate severe turbulence within an exchange regime that permits market flexibility in the exchange rate. Any conceivable exchange regime can be temporarily overwhelmed in stormy conditions—the more so if there are no cross-border or cross-currency breakwaters.

Though many commentators have yearned for an "optimal" exchange regime, no such regime exists. Appropriate exchange-rate policy is highly dependent on the context in which it is implemented. For an individual nation, no one regime can be best in all times and all circumstances.

Conventional wisdom sometimes asserts that the only viable options for a nation are the two extremes—either the pure flex of free floating or the hard fix of irrevocable pegs to one or more foreign currencies (for example, to one large country's major currency or to an actual currency union). That "corner-solution" view asserts that the middle ground of intermediate exchange regimes is bound to disappear over medium runs. Yet that view does not rest on sound analytical foundations or robust empirical evidence. And, again, no exchange-rate regime—none—can insulate a nation from financial turbulence and economic disruption if its macroeconomic and prudential-oversight policies are unsound.

The yearning for an ideal set of exchange-rate arrangements is misguided. The manner and degree of exchange-rate variability are not, in themselves, the financial policy issues of overriding importance. Home authorities should avoid a preoccupation with the choice of exchange regime and instead make their exchange-regime decisions jointly with decisions about the rest of home macroeconomic and financial-system policies. The highest priority should be placed on developing sound macroeconomic policies and ensuring high standards and competent prudential oversight for the nation's financial system.

To simplify an exposition of the policy trade-offs that bedevil this area, boil down the goals of macroeconomic and financial policies into three broad objectives. These three are, in effect, a distillation of the longer list of goals already summarized.

First, the nation would like to maintain economic and financial autonomy from the rest of the world. In particular it would prefer its central bank to pursue an unconstrained monetary policy. Second, the nation would like to avoid disorderly fluctuations in financial prices. In particular, because the external exchange value of the nation's currency is a financial price with pervasive effects throughout the economy and financial system, the nation would prefer exchange-rate stability. Finally, the nation would like to reap the many benefits associated with extensive financial integration with the rest of the world.

Textbook expositions label these three objectives an "impossible trilemma." The insight asserts that the three objectives are mutually incompatible. Any two of the three may be attainable. Extensive financial integration with the rest of the world and exchange-rate stability could be realized if the nation were to join a currency union and give up an independent monetary policy. Financial autonomy and exchange-rate stability could be achieved if the nation were to erect barriers to prevent cross-border financial transactions. If the exchange rate were allowed to fluctuate freely, it might be possible to have financial autonomy and widespread freedom for cross-border capital flows. But all three taken together are not mutually attainable. Further, the more the nation strives to attain any two of the three, the more it must surrender aspirations simultaneously to achieve the third.

To complicate matters further, home governing authorities confront a related trilemma. Because exchange-rate changes by themselves cannot insulate the home nation from monetary and financial shocks originating abroad, policy decisions face additional downside risks. While potentially a source of enhanced benefits, increasing cross-border integration further worsens the trade-offs that home policies must confront when navigating among multiple objectives. As Maurice Obstfeld argues, the increasing integration "raises the marginal value of additional tools of macroeconomic and financial policy. Unfortunately, the availability of such tools is constrained by a *financial* policy trilemma that is distinct from the monetary trilemma." This second trilemma complements the better-known monetary trilemma. "Specifically, countries must choose among national sovereignty over financial stability policy, policy integration into global financial markets, or financial stability—but they cannot have all three."[1]

Home authorities should regard the insights from both impossibility trilemmas as correct. And remember that, again, authorities are not required to be purist about their objectives.

---

1. Maurice Obstfeld, BIS Working Paper (January 2015); and Maurice Obstfeld and Alan M. Taylor, "International Monetary Relations: Taking Finance Seriously," *Journal of Economic Perspectives* (Summer 2017). See also Dirk Schoenmaker, *Governance of International Banking: The Financial Trilemma* (2013).

Rather than striving for the whole loaf of financial autonomy and the whole loaf of full freedom for cross-border financial transactions, the nation could surrender some of both objectives, aiming at half a loaf of autonomy and half a loaf of financial integration with the rest of the world. More generally, rather than striving for full attainment of any two of the three broad objectives, the nation may be better off aiming at some combined mixture of all three.[2]

Wise policy decisions avoid too simplified a view about trade-offs. Policymakers should not think in terms of purist choices. They need not wholly surrender their hopes for any of the three monetary-trilemma objectives (not to mention hopes for all of their more basic goals). Yes, they should sensibly stress the difficult nature of the trade-offs, not allowing themselves to believe that all the nation's goals are mutually compatible. But at best they should be eclectic and pragmatic in seeking a compromise combination of them.

Two other general points are pertinent. Once an overall coherent strategy and combination of goals has been decided, policymakers should articulate that strategy to both citizens and foreigners. When informed observers have an accurate grasp of a nation's overall strategy and the combination of goals that shape it, there is a much greater likelihood of actually implementing the strategy. In addition, policymakers need to understand that they must be prepared to adjust the strategy—and publicly explain

---

2. Some analysts even dislike the impossibility-trilemma simplification. Hélène Rey, for example, argued that mobile capital flows and vulnerability to external events cause strong cross-border transmission of global monetary conditions, even when exchange rates are flexible. These forces, she asserts, thus transform the traditional trilemma into a "dilemma," an "irreconcilable duo," which can push governing authorities to try to manage their capital inflows and outflows with direct controls. See Rey, "Dilemma not Trilemma: The Global Financial Cycle and Monetary Policy Independence" (2013).

the adjustments—if circumstances should substantially change the compromise combination of goals that best suits the nation's needs.

## Exchange-Rate Flexibility

Evidently, exchange-rate arrangements can be problematic. They are not an insulating device for a nation's economy and financial system. They are not a border buffer per se, though they obviously act as a complement.

If a nation has its own currency and a central bank manages its monetary and financial policies, there exists a definite preference for some discretionary flexibility in the exchange rates between its currency and foreign currencies.[3] The essential reason for this preference is straightforward: Exchange-rate flexibility brings additional smoothness and tractability into play for the adjustment of external imbalances. Changes in the external value of the nation's currency implicitly act as an additional tool of overall economic policy. If exchange-rate flexibility is not possible, some other instruments must be considered.

When some individual nations voluntarily peg their currency to a major foreign currency, their governing authorities may believe that the nation's circumstances justify such pegging. Other nations' policymakers may have chosen to participate in a currency union for reasons that are deemed, on balance, justified. For such nations, the change to having their own separate currency and an independent central bank would be legally and politically difficult.

---

3. It is a helpful shorthand, followed here, to use *the exchange rate* or *the external value of the home currency* as rough synonyms to refer to an aggregation of the various exchange rates linking the home currency to the multiplicity of relevant foreign currencies.

For nations that either cannot have or have forsworn exchange-rate flexibility, overall economic and financial policy is notably more difficult. Such nations must rely on alternative mechanisms instead of exchange-rate flexibility for adjustments of external imbalances. Willy-nilly, they have no other choice.

Why do exchange-rate variations facilitate the adjustment of external imbalances? Changes in home prices relative to foreign prices—and similarly, changes in home wages relative to foreign wages—can be powerful influences in adjusting external balances. Another powerful influence can be changes in home output relative to output produced abroad. For brevity, economists label changes in these ratios of home to foreign variables as cross-border adjustments in *relative prices*, in *relative wages*, and in *relative outputs*.

Effects brought about through changes in these relative ratios are central to understanding why exchange-rate flexibility can make adjustment of imbalances smoother and easier. Exchange-rate changes directly result, initially, in changes to relative prices and relative wages. Thus movements in the exchange value of the home currency, initially and, as it were, automatically, become translated into relative prices and relative wages. The resulting effects in the wider economy start to occur immediately, without as yet requiring further home policy actions. Changes in relative outputs and other variables will then occur as events evolve. But deliberate policy actions to alter home output relative to foreign output can come later. If the onus is on home policymakers to adjust home external imbalances, which is most often the case, the policymakers are likely to welcome the direct, faster changes in relative prices and relative wages initiated through exchange-rate changes. Adjustment of external imbalances that result from variations in relative prices/wages is quicker and easier for the home economy than changes in relative outputs.

If the home economy cannot experience the adjustment benefits of exchange-rate flexibility, a much larger part of the adjustment burden falls on other adjustment mechanisms. In particular, a larger part of the burden will probably fall on relative outputs than on relative prices and wages. The probability is higher that home incomes and home wealth will suffer more than if exchange-rate flexibility were part of the overall adjustment package.

Without easier and more prompt exchange-rate flexibility, changes in relative monetary and financial conditions are more difficult. Yes, nations that earlier chose to peg their currencies to a major currency can reverse gears; they can implement discrete devaluations or upvaluations to a new peg, or even unpeg altogether. But discrete changes are more likely to prove traumatic. The difficulties can be especially great if a nation belonging to a currency union abandons those arrangements, returning to its own separate currency and central bank. Because they are politically so costly, such discrete reversals of exchange-rate arrangements are infrequent.

The exchange-rate arrangements of European nations well illustrate the potential difficulties. In the twentieth century, with periods of stability alternating with wars and occasional crises, a majority of European nations had their own currencies and independent central banks. Exchange rates within Europe could and did change, often with interim disruptions. But then major decisions were jointly made in the final decade, culminating in the extended post–World War II period of European integration. The European Union (EU) was created and expanded in the 1990s. Many of the largest EU nations in 1999 established the "eurozone," with the euro as its common currency and the European Central Bank as its oversight financial institution. The United Kingdom and Sweden opted out of the eurozone, keeping their own currencies and central banks. Denmark negotiated a halfway house, keeping the Danish krone as its own legal currency but pegging the krone to the euro in a fixed-exchange-rate arrangement.

The eurozone is the world's most complex set of intermediate exchange arrangements. And it accordingly has complex procedures for adjusting external payment imbalances. With the euro as a single currency providing unambiguously for an absence of flexibility within the eurozone itself, adjustment of external imbalances within the eurozone occurs with the participants acting as in a currency union. But the exchange rates of the euro vis-à-vis non-eurozone currencies are flexible (primarily determined day to day by market traders). Hence the adjustment of external imbalances of the eurozone as an entirety with the rest of the world does benefit from the smoother and easier forces associated with some degree of exchange-rate flexibility.

The 1999 decision to create the euro currency union abruptly surrendered the ability of nations inside the eurozone to rectify internal zone imbalances through exchange-rate flexibility. Many economists at the time (myself included) had strong doubts about this surrender. While the introduction of the euro led to several years of temporary euphoria and large flows of capital from northern eurozone nations into southern eurozone nations, that temporary situation gave way in the second decade of the current century to troubled domestic instability, notably in Greece, Spain, Portugal, and Italy. Those southern nations experienced protracted weaknesses in output and sluggishness in restoring their competitiveness, not only within the eurozone but also in the wider world economy. The contrast in those years between the experiences of the Greek and Icelandic economies is instructive. Iceland (outside the eurozone, with its own currency) was able to regain external competitiveness sooner because its currency was devalued. Greece could not readily adjust its prices and wages relative to eurozone and non-eurozone nations, and had a deeper, more protracted crisis.

Issues of labor mobility also arise when analyzing the adjustment of external imbalances. Economic theory reminds us that labor and capital mobility across borders are to some degree a substitute for the free movement of goods and services. Both labor mobility and unrestricted trade potentially increase the effectiveness of resource allocation; more of one may help to compensate for less of the other. The architects of the European Union believed that there could be large economic benefits from workers moving across European borders, thereby allocating laborers to their most efficient uses. The formation of the eurozone, however, should have required policymakers to alter the way they perceive the substitutability of labor mobility and goods mobility. Because the de facto flexibility of exchange rates within the eurozone was abolished, relative internal prices and relative internal wages could no longer benefit from adjustments that were formerly smoother and easier. Hence there was subsequently a disproportionately higher need for the actual movement of workers themselves across internal borders. Changes in relative internal prices and relative internal wage rates could no longer play as significant and prompt a role. Paradoxically, just as uninhibited cross-border movements of people were to become less politically acceptable, they may have become more essential for smooth functioning of the eurozone.

Some limited generalizations sum up the advice about exchange-rate flexibility. A nation should use all the discretionary tools available to it. Additional degrees of freedom are almost always useful. A nation should not easily abandon discretionary maneuverability if and when it exists. All things considered, therefore, exchange-rate flexibility will be normally beneficial and should be welcomed when the circumstances permit. A counterpart generalization is that it will typically be preferable in a politically decentralized world for a nation to have a national currency, national monetary policies, and national prudential oversight over its financial system.

Some nations, especially smaller ones, may not have those governance choices. Altering their governance arrangements, as noted already, might not be possible in practice. So orderly exchange-rate flexibility might not be a practical option. The potential benefits of finding a way toward more orderly exchange-rate arrangements should probably never be altogether out of mind. But when alternative choices are definitely ruled out, the old cliché is inevitable: accept graciously what you do not have the power to change.

Smaller nations with their own currencies and central banks should be wary of abandoning the discretionary maneuverability permitted by exchange-rate flexibility. For nations that do not or cannot have separate currencies, their governing authorities should focus on wise deployment of the alternative mechanisms open to them for adjusting unwelcome imbalances.

Jurisdictions that cannot make use of exchange-rate flexibility may find themselves forced to consider direct controls on cross-border movements of financial capital.

Although from time to time some European and international pundits have pondered the idea of the eurozone splitting apart—returning some members to maintaining their own separate currencies—such a change would be dramatic in its political implications. As this book was going to press, such changes seemed to have a relatively low probability notwithstanding the augmented political turbulence that was buffeting the European Union.

As far ahead as one can imagine the evolution of Europe and the European Union, it would be ill-advised for the United Kingdom and Sweden to abandon their separate currencies and national central banks. This conclusion seems widely held within those nations, notwithstanding U.K. uncertainties about Brexit and the European Union. Danes might as well continue the fig leaf of pretending that Denmark might someday change its mind about keeping a rate pegged to the euro. Only soothsayers who are able to predict the outcome of Brexit uncertainties for Scotland can know whether Scotland will adopt the euro or eventually have its own new currency and a Scottish central bank.

The primary takeaway about exchange regimes is thus pragmatic. Nations that have an opportunity to make use of flexibility in exchange rates as a primary mechanism for adjusting external imbalances should prize that opportunity. An alphabetized list of prominent nations in this category includes Argentina, Australia, Brazil, Canada, Chile, China, Iceland, India, Indonesia, Iran, Israel, Japan, Mexico, New Zealand, Norway, Pakistan, the Russian Federation, Saudi Arabia, Singapore, South Africa, South Korea, Switzerland, Turkey, the United Kingdom, and the United States.

Once more the important caution: Even when there are beneficial effects stemming from exchange-rate flexibility, there is nonetheless still significant vulnerability and uncertainty associated with external financial openness. A responsible nation must craft a sensible balance between local autonomy and external openness, even if the escape valve of exchange-rate flexibility is available and working. Exchange-rate changes determined by market forces are not always orderly. They cannot reliably insulate economies from foreign monetary and financial shocks.

Behold, how good and how pleasant it is
for brethren to dwell together in unity!

*Psalm 133 (1), King James Version*

# 7. Cross-Border Governance and International Cooperation

The analysis of border buffers so far has sidestepped the possibilities of hostile interactions among national governing authorities. It also has sidestepped global issues such as the problem of climate change. Those omissions will now be corrected, coupled with an emphasis on the significance of international cooperation.

## Employ Border Buffers as Hostile Policy Instruments?

History is replete with conflicts among jurisdictions and among nations after the formation of nation-states. Wars have been the most extreme methods for coping with conflicts and for reconciling the tensions.

The profound defect of resolving disputes through the violence of war is that all nations, winners as well as losers, experience major losses of lives and resources. War is quintessentially a negative-sum game as a means for sorting out stressful policy differences.

Short of war, national governing authorities can be tempted to use changes in nonmilitary policy instruments as less violent methods of expressing hostility. The most localistic and selfish are willing to use those instruments, including border buffers, as if they were weapons. If a home nation's authorities are prepared to violate internationally agreed-upon rules and norms, they may be willing to initiate aggressive actions intended to increase home well-being at the deliberate expense of the well-being of foreigners. Such actions have often been labeled "beggar-thy-neighbor policies."

The aggressive use of border buffers and other nonmilitary policies as if they were weapons sometimes takes the form of policies announced as threats and then actually implemented. In other instances, aggressive policies may be threatened but with a hope that foreign responders will change their behavior before the aggressor nation needs to make the threats a reality. Some nations' political leadership may be most inclined to assert their interests aggressively when foreign nations are perceived as mild-mannered or have reputations for being cross-border cooperators. The most combative forms of aggressive behavior may be adopted by bigger and stronger nations who judge that they can get away with pushing smaller and weaker nations to submit to the more powerful aggressors.[1]

Suppose an aggressive home nation institutes higher tariffs or more restrictive quotas. Assume its goal is to protect local producers and workers at the expense of the well-being of foreign nations; it wishes to induce domestic consumers to switch from output produced abroad to domestically produced output. Assume the aggressor hopes that foreign nations will not retaliate by imposing incrementally more restrictive measures of their own. This type of hostile use of tariffs or quotas is most often

1. Border buffers used as hostile weapons are not instituted to rectify externalities and market failures (with those terms given their customary social science meanings).

encountered in the historical record. Prominent recent examples are the threats by the United States in 2018 to impose new tariffs on imports of steel, aluminum, solar panels, and washing machines from most countries. A further escalation took place in 2019 with U.S. tariffs on imports of consumer goods from China.

In contrast, an atypical use of higher tariffs or more restrictive quotas occurs if an aggressor nation's governing authorities threaten to institute the incremental tariffs or quotas not to achieve domestic effects at home, but rather to coerce a foreign nation to adopt particular policies sought by the aggressor. The foreign nation's policies sought by the aggressor might be unrelated to the foreign nation's cross-border trade. The aggressor's hope is that foreign governing authorities feel so coerced that they will adopt the designated policies (with the promise, explicit or implicit, that the aggressor authorities might then forestall adoption of its threatened new border buffers). A controversial prominent illustration was the U.S. threat in 2019 to impose new tariffs on imports from Mexico unless its governing authorities stopped migration through Mexico of illegal immigrants into the United States.

What are the consequences when an aggressor nation unilaterally adopts increased tariffs or more restrictive quotas? The aggressor's authorities may be pleased with themselves if, after their actions, they get away unscathed. But the more typical pattern is that the harmed, coerced foreign nations do not passively accept the aggression. In time, those most harmed tend to retaliate with offsetting hostile actions of their own, such as enhanced tariffs or quotas on imports from the aggressor nation.

No doubt all individual nations and their political leadership are capable to some degree of hostile, aggressive behavior. Common sense in avoiding strife is not all that common. Circumstances and preoccupations, changes of government, and unexpected crises all can trigger changes in behavior. And a corollary adage is pertinent: different strokes—bad or good—come from different folks.

History provides numerous examples where trade-policy border buffers were employed and responded to with hostility. Egregious cases occurred before and during the Great Depression years of the 1930s. The infamous Smoot-Hawley Tariff Act passed in June 1930 sharply raised tariffs on thousands of categories of U.S. imports. Members of Congress asserted that the tariffs would protect American businesses and farmers, thereby supporting the U.S. economy. Many foreign nations, some in response to Smoot-Hawley, retaliated with their own enhanced restrictions on their imports. Historians and economists widely agree that the tit-for-tat escalation of import restrictions in the 1930s contributed to a sharp decline in international trade, harmed rather than helped the U.S. and foreign economies, and seriously exacerbated the Depression.

The unambiguous verdict from the historical record damns the aggressive unilateral use of trade-policy border buffers. When trade policy actions take this form, the situation for all nations can easily become a negative-sum game in which most or all nations suffer net losses. Such negative-sum outcomes may not be as adverse as war itself, but the dynamic interactions among nations are analogous.

To put the matter in the opposite light, history strongly suggests that cooperative international agreements yield a better resolution of trade policy and border buffer disputes. The experiences of nations before, during, and after the Great Depression are again instructive. Tariff policies of the worlds' major nations were a mess in the 1920s, even characterized by Paul Krugman as a "cesspool of corruption and special interest politics" with respect to the United States.[2] Once the damages from the escalation of trade restrictions became better appreciated, a growing pushback occurred. The U.S. Congress, for example, passed the Reciprocal

2. Krugman (June 2019).

Trade Agreements Act in 1934, permitting tariffs to be reduced more easily and on a bilateral basis. International sentiment for cooperative trade agreements culminated in negotiations leading to the creation of new international institutions such as the International Monetary Fund (IMF) in 1944, the General Agreement on Tariffs and Trade (GATT) in 1947, and ultimately the World Trade Organization (WTO) in 1995.[3]

The potential significance of cooperative international agreements illuminates two of the general guidelines for border buffers summarized earlier. Again, home governing authorities should, in advance, evaluate likely reactions of foreign jurisdictions to prospective changes in home border policies. Adverse foreign reactions are especially possible when home decisions are introduced provocatively. And home authorities should carefully evaluate their reactions to unwanted policies implemented by foreign jurisdictions and avoid tit-for-tat self-defeating interactions with foreign governing authorities. An important aspect of good home decisions is a thoughtful differentiation of how foreign policy actions and home reactions affect home residents in transitory short-run ways versus effects that persist over a longer run.

Analysis of even the own-country effects of tariff increases is complex. Yes, incomes and jobs will initially be increased for home businesses and workers who produce home goods competitive with imports. But adverse effects can occur from decreases in home consumption of imports. The initial net effects for the home economy are difficult to predict because of numerous interdependencies within the domestic economy and the effects on relative prices channeled through the exchange rates of the home currency with foreign currencies. Essentially, much of the

---

3. Further passages discuss additional examples of successful international agreements. For references on the World Trade Organization, see, for example, Baldwin (2016) and VanGrasstek (2013).

higher import costs are passed through to domestic consumption. Higher home tariffs in practice are primarily a tax on home residents, not on foreigners. The net of costs and benefits to the home economy as a whole can be negative. It cannot be said with confidence that an aggressive unilateral raising of home tariffs is helpful to the home economy.

The net effects become that much harder to analyze after allowing for effects on producers, workers, and consumers resident in foreign nations. When and if foreign nations retaliate against the aggressive home tariff increases, the net cost calculations and their distribution across nations can change greatly. As with the widespread higher tariffs during the Great Depression, the resulting outcome can be a negative-sum game in which most or all nations suffer net losses.

A further analytical point to emphasize is that the cross-border interactions initiated by unilateral aggressive restrictions on trade are not exclusively economic. If nationalist localist policies threaten to accumulate, the issues of peace and political stability can also move to center stage.

At the time this book is written, it is much too soon to attempt a balanced assessment of tariff policy changes in the years 2017 to 2019. Archetypal illustrations of hostile disputes from the period were identified above because of their general significance. That period of hostile behavior accordingly warrants further mention.

The major tariff controversies stemmed from a growing hostility between China and the United States. Disputes between those two nations were perhaps inevitable given their increasing political, military, and economic rivalry, and the quantitative importance of their cross-border trade. The contentious dialogue often occurred between the top-level political leaders, President Xi Jinping and President Donald Trump. The United States and China each had complaints, some probably justifiable, about the other's trade and economic policies. The challenged policies included rule infringements about intellectual property, technology restrictions, and WTO procedures and norms. The disputes had often been exaggerated or misstated in public commentary. But there was general acknowledgment that the disputes belonged on the stage.

Not all the hostility and trade controversy stemmed from China and the United States. The United States also initiated adversarial discussions with Canada and European-Union nations. President Trump's statements consistently criticized and undermined the WTO. He faulted the policies and institutions of the European Union. He asserted unambiguous, unnuanced support of the U.K. position on Brexit negotiations with the European Union. He labeled the existing North American Free Trade Agreement (NAFTA) as "the worst trade deal the U.S. has ever signed" and then abrasively renegotiated with Canada and Mexico a new United States-Mexico-Canada Agreement (USMCA) that was similar to NAFTA.

The most regrettable mistake in tariff policies by the United States was the 2019 threat to progressively raise tariffs on U.S. imports from Mexico unless its authorities agreed to adopt dramatic measures to inhibit passage through Mexico of immigrants intending to cross the U.S. southern border illegally. This threat, a major departure from internationally accepted norms about legitimate and illegitimate justifications for tariff increases, was roundly criticized by foreign nations. President Trump withdrew the threat after Mexican authorities succumbed in part to the coercion.

Much will be said in coming years about the sad period of 2017 to 2019 and its worldwide failures in trade policies. One of its saddest trends was the sharp increase in hostile rhetoric and excessive localist behavior. The worst culprit, it is painful to note, was the United States—the single nation that above all others should have recognized its own deep interest in improving international collective governance. Instead of blowing the trumpet for the potential benefits of sensible norms and collective decisions, President Trump over and over again deliberately belittled the significance of international agreements and institutions. It is an easy prediction that future historians of world affairs will on this account denounce the 2017–2019 leadership of the United States.

A spirit of international comity and the embodiment of cooperative decisionmaking in international agreements are preconditions for stable international rules of law for trade policies. That same conclusion applies more generally for all types of border-buffer policies.

What is *comity*? Comity is an association of entities formed for mutual benefit. Comity is characterized by courtesy and considerate behavior toward others in the association. For better or worse, the planet is an association of nation-states. Cross-border comity avoids tit-for-tat spirals across borders that can lead to outcomes in which few if any individual nations are better off while many or most are definitely worse off. More generally, international comity avoids bad outcomes of negative-sum games among nations because it fosters better dispute resolution in a political environment characterized by cooperation. Its background conditions—its atmosphere—cultivate possibly better outcomes in which losses to most or all parties can be small and many parties can actually experience gains.

Ample historical evidence shows that international agreements can mitigate cross-border conflicts. Wise nations enter into such agreements precisely to help resolve the cross-border spillovers that cause conflicts in the first place. Again, the post–World War II institutions of GATT, the WTO, and the IMF reduced barriers to cross-border trade and finance, facilitating worldwide improvement in general well-being. International comity—in particular where it supports agreed-upon international norms for low tariffs and low quotas—is shown to be more beneficial than a free-for-all system without agreed-upon norms and dispute-resolution procedures.

Another thought to keep matters in perspective: This book focuses mostly on larger intergovernmental agreements and the international institutions they spawn. But that focus fails to highlight the multiplicity of private and smaller governmental arrangements. Though less discussed, those multiple other cross-border agreements are consequential. If one counts the total of international agreements and agreement updates in force, that number approached 200,000 toward the end of the first decade of the twenty-first century. The heterogeneity in design provisions in international law was "vast and shrewd," including those agreements dealing with duration, monitoring, punishment, escape, and withdrawal.[4]

## Global Climate Change: Progress Depends on International Cooperative Agreements

Ideas about internationally agreed norms and standards lead naturally to the topic of climate and environmental conditions. Global climate change is causing damaging market failures and public-goods externalities affecting the entire planet. Increased emissions of carbon dioxide and other greenhouse gases into the atmosphere are the quintessential cross-border spillovers, creating the problem of global warming of temperatures. Global warming is "the most significant of all environmental externalities. . . . It is particularly pernicious because it involves so many activities of daily life, affects the entire planet, does so for decades and even centuries, and, most of all, because none of us acting individually can do anything to slow the changes."[5, 6]

4. For a helpful overview of the multiplicity and complexity of agreement designs, see Barbara Koremenos, *The Continent of International Law: Explaining Agreement Design* (2016, chapter 1). The private-sector agreements include countless bilateral investment treaties (BITs) establishing legal terms and conditions for investments by nationals and companies of one nation in another nation (foreign direct investments, or FDIs).

5. The quote is from William Nordhaus, "Climate Change: The Ultimate Challenge for Economics" (June 2019), pp. 1991–2014. This article, Nordhaus's revised Nobel Prize lecture, summarizes many of the issues in a clear and insightful way.

6. Other overview references on global climate change include Liu, McKibbin, Morris, and Wilcoxen (2019); Metcalf (2019); Leonhardt (2019);

Carbon dioxide and other greenhouse gases emitted into the atmosphere in one part of the world spill over everywhere. Nothing at one nation's borders can prevent its emissions from affecting the atmosphere experienced by all. Therefore, policy actions to reduce emissions in an individual nation do not have their primary effects at home. Suppose a home nation were (atypically) to spend large amounts of its tax revenues to reduce domestic emissions. Atmospheric damages from those reductions would decline for the whole planet by the entire amount of the home nation's effort. However, only a small fraction of the beneficial reductions would be experienced as an improved atmosphere at home. The home nation is therefore likely to refrain from voluntarily using its resources to take actual steps to reduce emissions. The nation will be a "free rider" (see chapter 2), not making what should be its contribution to rectifying the planetary market failure. The nation may proclaim rhetorical endorsement for reductions of emissions. But in practice it is likely to rely on other nations to shoulder the costly expenses of doing so.

If there is no explicit cooperative agreement for nations to act together, the de facto result can be a noncooperative outcome with little reduction in emissions. In William Nordhaus's phrase, the practical message to nations about purely voluntary arrangements is to "speak loudly but carry no stick at all."

The actual market failure is still worse because the free riding is intergenerational. The current generation of adults today tends to tout the virtues of reducing emissions but nonetheless does little itself. Instead it passes remedial actions on to succeeding generations. But in practice it is today's children and grand-

---

McKibbin and Wilcoxen (2007, 2008). Reports from the United Nations Intergovernmental Panel on Climate Change (IPCC) are identified in a further footnote. For a gloomy perspective, see Wallace-Wells (2019).

children who will be most severely harmed by a greatly damaged global climate. Again, the individual incentives are biased against needed actions because the largest fraction of the beneficial consequences of emission reductions implemented by today's generation would ensue mostly in future decades.

When large and complex spillovers across national borders are absent, localist pluralism is less problematic. Wise home governing authorities can then focus primarily on the interests of home citizens. Good governance can block narrow or corrupt domestic efforts from promoting unhelpful domestic standards, lax environmental regulations, or protectionist trade policies.

When spillovers are great, however, narrowly nationalistic policies that eschew cross-border cooperation become counterproductive. Policies that try to foster the interests of a single nation, especially at the expense of others, lead to negative-sum games where outcomes for all nations are adverse.

As with trade border buffers, cooperation across borders can help a home nation avoid entanglement in a negative-sum game. Noncooperative inward-looking policies are thus markedly inferior for resolving global problems. And there is a partly favorable history. Yes, cooperative international agreements are difficult to design and negotiate. But they have been arranged frequently in the past.

A variety of strategies for ameliorating global climate change have long been proposed. Many advocate for direct taxation of the use of fossil fuels and carbon (that is, some form of a tax on the carbon price directly). Others suggest instituting so-called cap-and-trade arrangements for emissions permits. Still others promote subsidizing the development of innovative new technologies for producing alternative, low-carbon energy sources such as solar, wind, or water. Yet others support innovation in carbon-capture technologies (for example, man-made systems that sequester carbon dioxide in much the same way as natural carbon sinks such as plants, forests, oceans, and soil), and, alternatively, new regulations to diminish deforestation and other human behaviors that weaken the effects of the natural carbon sinks.

Support exists for combinations of the different strategies. Experts on climate-change issues, however, appear to support primary reliance on direct efforts for diminishing greenhouse gas emissions. Such measures would directly focus on abatement of these emissions by reducing the combustion of carbon fuels. Abatement strategies that include these measures may be the best hope for international progress in averting damages from global warming. To succeed, all combinations of strategies must somehow raise, directly or indirectly, the market price of carbon.

Many economists prefer focusing directly on the carbon price rather than on complex combinations of several strategies (which often directly discuss the quantities of emissions). These economists believe that the simplicity of focusing on the carbon price will prove decisive in achieving emission reductions. Other analysts argue instead that downplaying the necessary rise in carbon prices will prove more politically feasible. They assert that an emphasis on the mechanism of reducing emissions (raising the price of carbon) will attract greater political opposition than an emphasis on end-goal targets (reductions in the quantities of emissions).[7]

It is unclear which view about the political emphasis of strategies will ultimately have greater validity. All strategies (and combinations of strategies) are fraught with enormous political problems, especially within nations but also in international negotiations.

As a key example, consider the question of how the costs of alleviating global warning through abatement of emissions

---

7. See, for example, the overview article by David Leonhardt, "Economists have workable policy ideas for addressing climate change. But what if they're politically impossible?" (April 2019).

should be distributed across nations and regions. For simplicity, a few might argue that the costs incurred could be spread across nations in proportion to the size of their emissions. The more a nation emits, the more it should contribute to its share of world reductions; if a nation has grown strongly and increased its emissions rapidly, it should in turn reduce its carbon emissions correspondingly more.

Such a presumption is repellent to poorer parts of the world. Reducing the use of fossil fuels in poor, developing nations slows their growth, making it more difficult for them to lift their citizens out of poverty. From the perspective of those nations, richer nations that advocate large reductions in carbon dioxide emissions forget how much the rich nations' own earlier growth relied on energy derived from fossil fuels. The poor resent that they now should forego the advantages experienced earlier by the rich. Why should they, the poor, now be expected to share commensurately in today's costs of reducing emissions and improving the planetary atmosphere when the rich, at comparable stages of their own development, lavishly used carbon fuels and helped to create the current adverse climate changes? Needless to say, this question does not have easy or consensual answers. Such distribution and compensation issues, if not skillfully addressed and resolved, have the potential to completely undermine cooperative international agreements for mitigating global climate change.[8]

In fact the most critical point to stress is the need for en-

---

8. This point is stressed by Kemal Dervis and Sebastian Strauss, "The Real Obstacle for Climate Action" (August 2019), who argue that distributional issues are "the real obstacle to the ambitious policies needed to avert possibly catastrophic climate change." A similar point is made even more stridently by Bjørn Lomborg (August 2019). Lomborg and the Copenhagen Consensus Center argue that "concerned activists want the world to abandon fossil fuels as quickly as possible. But it will mean slowing the growth that has lifted billions out of poverty and transformed the planet. That has a very real cost."

hanced international cooperation. The slowing of climate change requires collaborative global actions nurtured in a dialogue underpinned with international comity. The point cannot be made too strongly: Collaborative actions of some type, eventually yielding binding international agreements, are the only path for hopeful progress. As cross-border flows among nations increase in relative importance, international collective action becomes more and more essential through time.

The steps for reducing emissions simply will not be forthcoming if individual nations are expected only to take voluntary steps without collaborative commitments from other nations. Free-riding disincentives will defeat voluntary efforts. If a safe and congenial climate for the planet is to be attained, it will have to be through coordinated actions by coalitions of nations agreeing on committed strategies to reduce emissions and backstopped by enforcement mechanisms that penalize nations initially unwilling to cooperate.

At least initially, of course, agreements need not include all nations. But it is essential that the largest contributors to greenhouse gas emissions—most of the dozen largest emitting nations—be seen to participate. The first-best plan—obviously not yet attainable—would be for those major nations to cooperate by pledging to adopt binding commitments and detailed agreements that embody enforcement mechanisms. And eventually, more and more nations would have to step up to some degree; otherwise a larger fraction of the citizens of the main emitters is likely to withdraw from supporting the needed collaborative efforts.

Many economists and some policymakers have recently discussed a possible enforcement mechanism that could mitigate the hesitancy of nations to participate initially. This mechanism, an internationally designed "border carbon adjustment" (BCA), would tax imports into cooperating economies from nonparticipant nations where carbon leakages are greater. The rate of the

BCA tax would be commensurate with the estimated amount of carbon dioxide incorporated in the production of the imports. The existence of the BCA could allow collaborating participants to pursue more ambitious climate-change policies because their domestic industries would not be competitively undermined by foreign suppliers in nonparticipant nations not yet adequately reducing carbon emissions.[9]

Sadly, international comity in this area has been only faintly visible. Progress in slowing climate change has been, at best, extremely modest. As Nordhaus emphasizes, "The policies taken to date fall far short of what is necessary to slow climate change sufficiently to meet international goals."[10] In 2018–2019, more alarm bells sounded: estimates of likely further damages in the shorter run increased notably.[11] Those shifts in evidence further reduced the plausibility of gradualist approaches being sufficient and greatly strengthened the case for much faster and bolder forms of mitigation. A few signs emerged suggesting a gradual strengthening of international norms to support more vigorous international cooperation. But national authorities were still a very long way from imagining and then adopting collaborative arrangements that will slow the ominous march of climate change.

Existing international agreements have been almost so weak as to warrant being called cosmetic. The Kyoto Protocol of 1997,

9. Proposals for a border carbon adjustment (BCA) tax were endorsed by thousands of economists in a joint 2019 statement (see article in the *Wall Street Journal*, "Economists' Statement on Carbon Dividends," January 17, 2019). The European Union in 2019 was considering adoption of one version of a BCA (see Henrik Horn and Andre Sapir, "Border Carbon Tariffs: Giving Up on Trade to Save the Climate?" [August 29, 2019]). BCA tax proposals of course raise numerous detailed issues of design and cooperative implementation. See, for example, Sam Lowe (September 24, 2019).

10. Nordhaus (June 2019), pp. 2007–15.

11. See, for example, reports from the UN Intergovernmental Panel on Climate Change (May 2019, August 2019, September 2019).

the first major collaborative effort, was long on helpful rhetoric but had only weak promises of future actions. It notably had no meaningful enforcement mechanisms. Similarly, the 2015 Paris Accord that replaced the 1997 Kyoto Protocol was *"uncoordinated and voluntary"* (Nordhaus's emphasis). Its policies, even if undertaken, would not limit climate change to its agreed targets. "Moreover, while countries agree to make best efforts, there are no penalties if they withdraw or fail to meet their obligations. The world is therefore just where it stood in 1994, recognizing the dangers of climate change without effective policies to stop it."[12]

To highlight the most egregious illustration, consider the flabbergasting position of U.S. president Donald Trump on climate-change policies! In 2017, Trump announced that the United States intends to withdraw completely from the Paris Accord agreement (the actual withdrawal to occur in November 2020). The United States, a leading world power, delivered a symbolic bombshell—one diametrically opposed to what would make sense for the United States alone as well as for encouraging appropriate cooperation and comity among the rest of the world's nations. The Paris Accord is imperfect in numerous respects. It badly needs improving adjustments. But it is a colossal failure of leadership for the economically strongest high-emitting nation in the world to withdraw from cooperative participation.

### Cross-Border Comity, Historical Progress

Short-run despair about climate change is virtually unavoidable. But despair can be overdone. And it can inhibit fruitful cooperation to redress the causes of despair. Historical progress often swings like a pendulum. Periods of promising cooperation alternate with periods of retreat.

In this section, I thus turn to instances of achievements in

---

12. Nordhaus (2019, pp. 2007–2015).

international cooperation where progress has been encouraging rather than discouraging.

Antarctica is a continent but not a nation-state. Its governance is manifested through international agreements, not via institutions directly analogous to a national government. Antarctic governance is therefore a unique manifestation of planetary cooperation.

The arrangements made for the purpose of regulating relations among states in the Antarctic are known as the Antarctic Treaty System. The core of the arrangement is the Antarctic Treaty itself. The original parties to the treaty were the twelve nations active in the Antarctic during the International Geophysical Year project in 1957 to 1958. The treaty was signed by the twelve nations in 1959 and entered into force in 1961. As of 2019, fifty-four nation-states were participants, twenty-nine of which (including all twelve original signatories) had consultative voting status.[13] Antarctica is defined as all of the land and ice shelves south of 60°S latitude.

The Antarctic Treaty System sets aside Antarctica as a scientific preserve and supports scientific research, which is the main activity on the continent and surrounding seas. Ongoing experiments are conducted by scientists from many nations. The treaty system prohibits military activities, nuclear explosions, and nuclear waste disposal.[14] It bans mineral mining and protects the continent's ecozone. Activities within Antarctica are coordinated through the Council of Managers of National Antarctic Programs (COMNAP), founded in 1989. The various national Antarctic organizations and scientific groups are members of COMNAP.

13. The original twelve nations were Argentina, Australia, Belgium, Chile, France, Japan, New Zealand, Norway, South Africa, the United Kingdom, the United States, and the Soviet Union.

14. The treaty was the first arms control agreement established during the Cold War.

They review operations, share information, and provide a forum for dealing with logistical issues.

The Antarctic Treaty System, the implementation through COMNAP, and additional protocols and agreements associated with them appear to be models of consultations and negotiations handled smoothly and skillfully. Cross-border comity is the foundation of the agreements. It is very widely believed by scholars, and even by a large majority of national politicians, that the 1959 Antarctic Treaty "succeeded remarkably well in its first 50 years." The Treaty was elegant in its simplicity of only fourteen articles that would provide the basis for governance of nearly 10 percent of the Earth "for peaceful purposes only." Territorial issues were set aside. Research activities became

> the criterion for nations to consult on matters of common interest and to make decisions by consent of all parties. . . . With science as a tool of diplomacy, the Antarctic Treaty System has provided lessons that are relevant to the governance of transboundary systems as well as the other international spaces beyond sovereign jurisdictions (i.e., outer space, the deep sea, and the high seas) that together cover nearly 70% of the Earth's surface. With vision and hope for the future, the challenge of the Antarctic Treaty Summit was to identify and assess these science-policy lessons of international cooperation that have enabled both the flexibility and the resilience of the Antarctic Treaty.[15]

It is true that intergovernmental cooperation in the particular context of Antarctica was made easier by two facts: The continent

---

15. The quotations are from the preface to the compendium survey of the literature on Antarctica by the Smithsonian Institution after the 2009 Atlantic Treaty Summit; see Paul Arthur Berkman, Michael A. Lang, David W. H. Walton, and Oran R. Young, eds., *Science Diplomacy: Antarctica, Science, and the Governance of International Spaces* (2011). In addition to this key reference, a large amount of scholarly literature about Antarctica and the Antarctic Treaty System is readily available online.

did not have a native human population, and no indigenous governing authority existed to represent established "local" interests. Even so, the Antarctic achievements seem highly commendable. They are a landmark example of international cooperation.

The Montreal Protocol is a set of global treaty arrangements to protect the stratospheric ozone layer by phasing out the production and consumption of ozone-destroying substances. The substances targeted are chlorofluorocarbons (CFCs), including hydrochlorofluorocarbons (HCFCs). These dangerous substances are halogenated hydrocarbons containing chlorine or bromine. (Substances containing only fluorine do not harm the ozone layer.) These substances, as well as carbon dioxide and methane, are greenhouse gases that contribute to slowing the rate at which the Earth loses heat to space, thereby increasing the planet's surface temperature (the radiative forcing of climate change).

The treaty was negotiated in August 1987, entered into force in 1989, and has been revised multiple times in the two subsequent decades. It contains special phase-in provisions for developing countries.[16] As of 2018, essentially all nation-states in the world were participants in the Montreal Protocol and its associated arrangements.

As a result of the Montreal Protocol, the atmospheric concentrations of the dangerous CFCs and related chlorinated hydrocarbons have either leveled off or decreased. The ozone hole in Antarctica has been slowly recovering. Developed nations have been reducing their consumption of HCFCs and were to completely phase them out by 2020. Developing nations agreed to start their phaseout process for HCFCs in 2013 and are to follow a stepwise reduction until a complete phaseout by 2030. Climate projections now widely indicate that the ozone layer may return to 1980 levels sometime after 2050.

16. The Multicultural Fund for the Implementation of the Montreal Protocol exists to assist developing nation parties adopt the protocol.

The Montreal Protocol is therefore another notable illustration of successful international agreements addressed to global externalities. With its widespread adoption and implementation, it is the first global cooperative regime to achieve the status of universal ratification. It has been praised as an example of exceptional international cooperation and "perhaps the single most successful international agreement" in the twentieth century.[17]

As a final window into the presence and absence of cross-border comity, return to the financial vulnerability of individual nations and the world financial system. Prudential oversight to promote financial stability and prevent disruptions to credit and other financial services is centrally important within national jurisdictions. But it is no less important internationally. Despite occasional steps backward, recent decades have witnessed significant progress in international collective action in financial areas.

Still greater cooperation on many financial issues will be gradually needed over time. This complex of issues is sometimes labeled "architectural reform" of the utilities infrastructures of financial systems. Top priorities include fostering improvements in the prudential oversight of financial activities and the associated design and monitoring of financial standards; upgrading the supranational surveillance of cross-border traffic regulations; and improving intergovernmental financial intermediation for better cooperative management of financial crises (contingent provision of emergency lending). Oversight occurs at multiple levels. Macroprudential oversight—systemic supervision and regulation of entire markets and groups of financial institutions—has received enhanced attention. Microprudential oversight entails

17. The quotation is from Kofi Annan, Secretary-General of the UN from 1997 to 2006. The quote and projections about future progress in reducing the ozone hole are from the recent Wikipedia article on the Montreal Protocol. For detailed references and analysis, see, for example, Cumberland, Hibbs, and Hoch, eds. (1982) and Barrett (1994, 2003).

supervision and regulation of the safety and soundness of individual financial institutions. The underlying goals of both levels of oversight are the maintenance of financial stability and the prevention of economic and financial crises—prosperity management rather than crisis management.[18, 19]

A strong framework for microprudential oversight promotes the safety and soundness of individual firms. But relying only on microprudential oversight is not enough. Microprudential policies on their own could even increase system-wide risks if the behavioral interactions among all financial institutions are not considered.[20] Structural macroprudential tools build resilience to fragilities in financial markets and adverse events in business cycles. An example is the imposition of higher capital ratios for systemically important lenders, where systemic lenders are deemed to pose higher risks to the entire financial system. Limits on loan-to-value ratios or on debt-service-to-income ratios for mortgage debtors are examples

18. See Bryant, *Turbulent Waters* (2003) and *Crisis Prevention and Prosperity Management for the World Economy* (2004), for more detailed discussions of these financial issues.

19. For an insightful collection and analysis of empirical data for cross-border financial relationships, see Lane and Milesi-Ferretti (2007, 2011, 2018). See also Bertaut, Bressler, and Curcuru (2018).

20. My Brookings colleagues Kadiija Yilla and Nellie Liang stress the following example: "In a microprudential framework, the ability of a bank to increase its capital to meet regulatory requirements is seen as favorable, without regard to how this is accomplished. But a bank that needs to increase its capital ratio (measured as a percentage of its assets) can either raise new capital or decrease assets (loans). When bank losses are increasing because the economy is weak and bank capital ratios are falling, the difference between the two approaches is consequential. If every firm were to decrease assets instead of raise capital, that action would lead to a substantive contraction of credit and cause the economy to weaken further. A macroprudential approach, in contrast, would assess and control for the mechanism that banks would implement to reach their required capital ratio, essentially encouraging them to raise capital rather than pull back on lending."

applied to borrowers. Cyclical macroprudential tools aim to increase systemic resilience in anticipation of economic downturns, thereby lessening reductions in the supply of credit if and when the downturns come to pass. The buffers established by Countercyclical Capital Requirements (CCRs) are an example; they can require banks to increase their capital cushions during expansions when systemic risks are rising and then allow release of the buffers in downturns to help absorb losses.

Key international institutions with financial oversight responsibilities are the IMF, the Bank of International Settlements (BIS), and the Organisation for Economic Cooperation and Development (OECD). De facto, the BIS functions as a central bank for nations' central banks. It also serves as a locus for subsidiary and coordinated financial activities (as does the IMF). Among the important associated organizations hosted by the BIS is the Financial Stability Board (FSB). Three other BIS-hosted financial organizations with responsibility for coordinating prudential oversight and supervisory functions include the Basel Committee on Banking Supervision (BCBS), the Committee on the Global Financial System (CGFS), and the Committee on Payments and Market Infrastructures (CPMI). Separate international organizations include the International Organization of Securities Commissions (IOSCO), the International Association of Insurance Supervisors (IAIS), the International Accounting Standards Board (IASB), and the Financial Action Task Force (FATF). The FATF's objectives are "to set standards and promote effective implementation of legal, regulatory, and operational measures for combating money laundering, terrorist financing and other related threats to the integrity of the international financial system." Merely listing these international organizations gives a glimpse into the scope of collaborative activities in these financial areas.

The Financial Stability Board (FSB) was established in April 2009 as a strengthened successor to the Financial Stability Forum

(FSF), which dates back to 1999. The goals of the FSB are enhancement of cooperation among the various national and international supervisory bodies and international institutions for the purpose of promoting stability in the international financial system. Authorities responsible for financial stability in large nations and significant financial centers (such as central banks, treasuries, and supervisory agencies) are formal members of the FSB. So are international groupings of regulators and supervisors engaged in developing standards and codes of good practice. So, too, are international financial institutions charged with the surveillance of domestic and international financial systems, and the monitoring and implementation of standards.

The FSB (earlier the FSF) and its related organizations have addressed numerous issues of financial standards, including sector-specific minimum standards. Many statements and documents have been published under its auspices.[21]

Simultaneously with the activities of the FSB and its organizations, national governments themselves established multiagency financial stability committees (FSCs). Prior to the 2007–2009 global financial crisis, twelve nations already had an FSC. That number increased to forty-seven by 2018. These FSCs almost always include central banks and prudential regulators, but the newer committees also tend to include representatives of the elected government, such as the ministry of finance. The powers of FSCs vary across nations. Only one quarter are enabled to take actions. The others appear mainly to facilitate information sharing and policy coordination across the multiple agencies while the agencies retain the power to set policies.[22]

---

21. The FSB website, with numerous documents and large amounts of information, is found at www.fsb.org.

22. For discussion, see Rochelle Edge and Nellie Liang, "New Financial Stability Governance Structures and Central Banks" (February 2019).

Positive steps forward in the area of macroprudential over-sight have been encouraging.[23] A small example seems worthy of mention here, not so much because of its inherent significance but rather as a token of the farsighted advances to be hoped for in the turbulent years ahead. In late 2019 the Bank of England released a draft discussion paper asking for outside comments on a "2021 biennial exploratory scenario on the financial risks from climate change." The scenario is part of the bank's efforts to test the resilience of the largest banks and insurers in regard to the risks associated with different possible climate scenarios and, more broadly, the world financial system's exposures to climate-related risks.[24]

Cross-border cooperation was especially needed, and for-tunately was forthcoming, during the global financial crisis of 2007–2009. Many specific acts of consultation and collaboration supported efforts to mitigate the damaging effects. The rapid expansion and aggressive use of swap networks among central banks (such as those of the U.S. Federal Reserve) were instru-mentally reassuring. Ex post evaluations of the crisis responses by most governments have been widely supportive. A broad ret-rospective concluded that

> the totality of the evidence suggests that the interventions, though far from perfect, prevented a second Great Depression.

23. For general commentaries on recent developments, see, for example, Donald Kohn, "Macroprudential Policy: Implementation and Effectiveness" (2016); and Nellie Liang, "Rethinking Financial Stability and Macroprudential Policy" (2017).

24. The Bank of England asked for outside comments on the design of the exercise and welcomes feedback from firms, their counterparties, climate sci-entists, economists, and other industry experts. The final Bank of England sce-nario framework was to be published in the second half of 2020, and the results of the exercise were to be published in 2021. See Bank of England, Financial Policy Committee and Prudential Regulation Committee (December 2019).

Research on the individual actions taken show they were effective in that they moved key outcome measures, such as risk spreads, and ultimately credit, output, and employment, in the desired direction. However, while the economy performed substantially better than might be expected based on previous financial crises, the actions were not able to prevent a severe recession and a weak recovery.[25]

One suggested principle for international standards is that no nation should be accorded the full benefits of participation in the world financial system and its supporting international organizations if that nation persists in maintaining standards and prudential oversight for financial activity that are weak relative to world minimum standards. A mild but sometimes effective option is to cooperate in an international "name and shame" policy of identifying renegade jurisdictions.

Early in the twenty-first century, strengthened prudential and tax standards were encouraged for offshore financial centers (OFCs; see chapter 4). The cooperative pressures implemented through the Financial Stability Board used the so-called name and shame approach. Nations meriting criticism were named individually in published reports and press releases. The FATF and the OECD subsequently followed a similar approach in publicly identifying nations that were "tax havens" or "noncooperative in the fight against money laundering."

Given the natural hesitation in international discussions to point fingers at specific nations, the FSB, FATF, and OECD ac-

25. The quotation is from Nellie Liang, "Eight Lessons for Fighting the Next Financial Crisis" (2018). A revised version of Liang's paper is included in the Bernanke-Geithner-Paulson-Liang compendium, *First Responders: Inside the U.S. Strategy for Fighting the 2007–2009 Global Financial Crisis* (2020). For an insightful first-person account of the crisis, see Ben Bernanke, *The Courage to Act: A Memoir of a Crisis and Its Aftermath* (2015).

tivities were commendably assertive. I bring up their name and shame approach only as one of many possible illustrations of international cooperative monitoring of financial issues. Such constructive steps toward international collective governance were not politically feasible in the twentieth century.

To summarize: Intergovernmental cooperation on financial issues has been evolving on multiple fronts. The direction of change has been largely positive. Progress appears genuine and significant. This optimistic trend deserves more widespread attention and commendation than it typically receives.

This chapter has grappled with numerous issues about border buffers, cross-border governance, and international cooperation. Simplified answers to most questions are not wise or plausible. Only from a sweeping perspective can one assert general guidelines. Yet a few basic points can be repeated with confidence.

Is it satisfactory for individual nations to use border buffers as hostile policy instruments (as in the U.S. use of tariff buffers under President Trump's administration)? Or are border buffers better employed as catalysts for cross-border comity grounded in cooperative international agreements—such as for climate change or for financial stability? How much localism in national policies is appropriate?

The overview answer for all sector-specific areas is unambiguous. Actively hostile behavior is not only unwelcome but often counterproductive. Some degree of localism is valid for home nations. That posture alone justifies, and should shape, the establishment and maintenance of border buffers. But, just as important, evidence—strong evidence—of collective cooperation with outside nations is essential as well. Collaborative cross-border support for international standards and comity are needed for nations to have ballast to function successfully in a highly integrated world.

Localist postures by individual nations can all too easily drift toward an anticosmopolitan extreme. Conduct that is, or even can be interpreted as, inimical to rules of international law can damage cooperative, peaceful relations among nations. International agreements and standards—cross-border comity—are needed to constructively restrain excesses of local diversity.

As suggested by the examples of Antarctica and the Montreal Protocol, further advances in cross-border comity are certainly possible. Thank goodness for the reassurance provided by history. For a sustainable, orderly evolution of the planet, most of all for mitigating the horrific potential damages from global warming, such evolutionary progress is mandatory. Our grandmothers were almost always right: When things seem impossible but there is a will, a way can be found.

**Medio tutissimus ibis.** (Go most safely by the middle way.)
*Advice given by Phoebus to the impetuous Phaeton,*
*Ovid,* Metamorphoses, *Book II*

# 8. Summing Up: Crafting a Balanced Compromise

This book addresses trade-off choices posed by geographical borders for the multiple governing jurisdictions of our higgledy-piggledy planet. The analysis highlights prominent features of the world landscape as a whole. As foreshadowed at the outset, it suppresses second-order details, as if evaluating from the flight of an eagle high overhead.

The survey began with analytic fundamentals. It reviewed the benefits of external openness, the associated costs and risks, how the benefits and costs are distributed, and the tensions between external openness and local autonomy. It then explored the differing perspectives of insider localists and outsider cosmopolitans within nations. Those two contrary outlooks, looking only inward and looking only outward, can pull apart the middle ground.

It next analyzed border buffers—harbor breakwaters, separation fences—that can provide frictions at national borders. In addition to buffers that affect trade and finance, the text tackled the problems associated with migration of people across borders. Hard questions about buffers were asked. Should a nation prefer localist diversity or "a level playing field"? Should the world community seek international minimum standards?

Exchange-rate arrangements were the next topic. The emphasis of the analysis was on how the presence or absence of exchange-rate flexibility influences adjustments to nations' external imbalances.

Finally, attention was devoted to examples of whether and how enhanced international agreements can improve cross-border governance. The book recommends that individual nations not aggressively wield tariffs or other border buffers as hostile policy instruments to coerce the behavior of foreign authorities. Could international cooperation improve enough to support progress in ameliorating the dangers of global climate change? Could it mitigate dangers from financial instability? Do nations have enough foresight to use border buffers as catalysts for cross-border comity and gradually stronger international agreements? The answers to those questions can and should be yes.

The primary conclusion of the book—and its dominant theme—is that trade-off tensions between local autonomy and external openness are best managed by middle-ground governance choices. Exploring the middle ground requires staying well away from the extremes of rigid localism and unfettered openness. The middle ground requires identification of compromise combinations.

Trade-offs between incompatible goals are inescapable. Moving closer toward one of two competing goals typically requires—requires!—moving away from the other. Some external openness must be sacrificed to achieve more local autonomy. Some autonomy must be surrendered to benefit from greater openness.

Finding compromise combinations for an intermediate middle ground is stressful. Appropriate compromises must incorporate a nation's specific characteristics and its current and prospective circumstances. Governing authorities need to craft wise trade-offs among all of a nation's goals, designing suitable compromise combinations rather than seeking a purist pursuit of only some subset. No one middle-ground stance can be right for all circumstances and all times. As a nation's economy and polity evolve, adjustments and experimentation are required.

The individuals and organizations within a nation that are most needed to identify the middle ground are "in-betweeners." An in-betweener perceives geographical belonging neither as a "localist-somewhere" nor as a "cosmopolitan-anywhere." In a successfully governed nation, the voices of the in-betweeners are more prominent and better heard. Localist extreme attitudes, reflecting rigid anticosmopolitan identities, are too distant from a middle ground. Unquestioning procosmopolitan identities are too distant in the opposite direction.

In-betweeners are much less likely to confuse de jure sovereignty with de facto autonomy. They understand that the true trade-off is between de facto local autonomy and external openness, that de jure sovereignty can be irrelevant, and that a nation reaping benefits from its openness may wisely accept reductions in its de facto autonomy.

Consensus and loyalty within a nation often lead to cohesion of views. Cohesion tames and shapes disruptive forces. It often fosters compromise. Centrifugal forces pulling some parts of a jurisdiction away from a middle-ground center must not be so strong as to undermine governance. Centripetal forces within a nation benefit from local nurture. Yet consensus, loyalty, and cohesion can be double-edged swords. Cohesion can be excessive. National loyalty, if extreme in the form of "my nation first—period," can harm fundamental national interests. Extreme and unbalanced cohesion can easily generate counterproductive tensions with foreign nations.

At best, cohesion among insiders and openness to the outside are both beneficial. Policymakers should encourage the voices of in-betweeners, thereby pulling the national center of gravity toward the middle ground. A middle-ground balance should be struck between active support of "me and mine" and wise cooperation with "them and theirs."

Looking in the rear-view historical mirror, cohesion in many societies was easier because of less pluralism and more homogeneity. Yet diverse polities today have no effective choice but to look ahead, not backward to renewed homogeneity. How can current polities lead to more cohesion despite the difficulties? Many people feel more cohesion with those who they perceive share their identity. But diversity and heterogeneity are facts of life. The practical challenge is to make all citizens, including newer ones, appear to each other as fellow citizens who share some basic identity.

The pervasive trend of increasing integration, evident for several centuries, has continued into the twenty-first century. Always powerful in its economic implications, the intensifying integration has had growing social and cultural implications. Interactions across geographical borders—typically characterized as "globalization"—have grown more rapidly than interactions among domestic residents. Scientific, technical, social, and cultural changes, especially information and communications technology, have sharply reduced the effective distances between nations. Policies and practices that traditionally inhibited cross-border transactions have been relaxed or dismantled. Nations thus have experienced greater external openness and growing interdependence. As the mouse in Franz Kafka's "A Little Fable" observed: "Alas, the whole world is growing smaller every day."[1]

Though less significant than in the past, national borders still have enormous salience. Available empirical evidence strongly refutes the generalization that cross-border economic linkages have intensified to the point that they are, after taking due account of distance, as tight as those within individual nations.

1. Franz Kafka's "A Little Fable" ("Kleine Fabel") first appeared in *Beim Bau der Chinesischen Mauer* in 1931. The first English translation, by Willa and Edwin Muir, was published by Martin Secker (London) in 1933.

Without doubt, national borders can be, and increasingly are, transcended for numerous types of electronic transactions, information flows, and cultural exchanges. It is a far-fetched exaggeration, however, to assert that national borders are dissolving.

Territoriality and geographical distance will not be superseded. Only for a tiny minority of the world's individuals can a few dimensions of economic and social life be accurately described as global. Yes, those dimensions are becoming gradually more salient. They are affecting more individuals. However, for most people in most jurisdictions in most parts of their lives, "global" labels mislead more than they inform. A thoughtful approach to governance choices for individual jurisdictions, nations, and for the entire world should eschew sweeping generalizations about globalization. The focus instead should be on the higgledy-piggledy status of the planet as it actually exists.

Increasing integration has brought, and will continue to bring, many benefits. But it also brings significantly enhanced risks and costs. Greater external openness and interdependence augments tensions. Not only is the world smaller, but also abrasiveness is closer at hand. The essential analytical point is that heightened spillovers across borders intensify pressures, both beneficial and detrimental, on cross-border interactions. And pressures then intensify for international cooperation. The heightened pressures for incremental collective action are a progressively salient feature of the world polity.

A second underlying theme of this book is the related trade-off between decentralized decisions and cooperative decision-making. The core of governance itself, as emphasized at the outset, is to identify and sustain compromise decisions for collective action.

This deep trade-off is essentially the same one that my Brookings colleague Arthur Okun emphasized decades ago in his analysis of equality and efficiency. Government actions to promote equality, and equality of opportunity, require cooperative decisions by governing authorities. Deliberate redistributions of economic welfare can partially rectify inequality. But government redistributive actions override markets, which are characterized by decentralized decisions made by numerous independent agents. Because markets are often efficient, overriding them can be costly. Compromises are necessary to find a middle ground. Okun's memorable conclusion was that "the market needs a place, and the market needs to be kept in its place."[2]

My book has been inspired by Okun. I recast the issues, however, in a more encompassing way. Okun's analysis dealt only with the single nation of the United States. The planet comprises some two hundred nations, with cultures and institutions that are much more heterogenous than within the United States alone. Even though dramatic changes have further integrated the planet, no less than before now a middle ground must be found between decentralized and cooperative decisions. For some important purposes now, the relevant decentralized decisions must be made by nation-states. The needed collective actions must be organized by explicit international agreements catalyzed by international institutions.

This book, accordingly, has required digging into the cross-border dimensions of the trade-offs between decentralized national actions and cooperative centralized decisions. The world into which we are navigating—like the metaphorical motorway in the book's introduction—is, alas, messy and accident-prone. There is no better choice than to cautiously steer near the middle of the road ahead, staying away from the ditches on either side, avoiding accidents amid the helter-skelter traffic. Border buffers

---

2. Arthur M. Okun, *Equality and Efficiency: The Big Tradeoff* (2015, p. 119). The quote is from Art's concluding paragraphs. Okun was keenly aware of international complications but omitted them from his analysis. The original publication date of Okun's book was 1975; the 2015 edition includes a 1977 article titled "Further Thoughts on Equality and Efficiency."

are, to a limited extent, our seat belts, airbags, and reinforced bumpers. The road itself, at regional and worldwide levels, could benefit from improved guardrails.

Whatever the particulars of the middle-way routes followed by individual nations, their governing authorities should collectively support norms and procedures for cross-border rule-of-law comity. Progressively stronger international institutions should be part of that comity. The details of national routes should sustain dispute-resolution arrangements that resolve major differences among nations. Internationally agreed-upon mechanisms should discourage excessively selfish, localist behavior. The two loyalties of moderate localism and moderate encouragement of international comity both should find overlapping support within individual nations. Neither should be demoted at the expense of the other.

The regional and global high-level needs for increased collective action have emerged strongly in recent decades. Yet perceptions of the needs among national governments and consensuses about possible actions have been slow in forming. In numerous instances, compromise trade-offs have not yet been reached. Decisions, when taken, have often only been timid.

And there are grounds for pessimism. The planet's biggest collective crises foreseeable over the longer run—think again of climate change, nuclear proliferation, and poorly managed cross-border migration—loom ominously. At the end of the second decade of the twenty-first century, tensions were evident in all directions. Political leadership was disappointing in so many nations, including (an incomplete list) Italy, Poland, the United Kingdom, Turkey, Venezuela, Brazil, Russia, Myanmar, China, and the United States. My own nation after 2017 seemed to depreciate its vision (temporarily, we hope) of an "American dream" that provides social justice and equal-opportunity access for all. Sadly, the United States under the Trump presidency undermined rather than facilitated international agreements and institutions.

I am near the end of my own life. Despite discouragement, sometimes even despair, I refuse to leave the scene with pessimism. Political leaders and we who support them can do better. For the sake of our grandchildren, and our grandchildren's grandchildren, we must do better, throughout the world.

The preceding pages, as in my earlier publications, argue for compromise and pragmatic incrementalism. That is an optimistic approach to the evolution of international collective governance. Pragmatic incrementalists are in-betweeners in spirit. They seek the middle-ground routes along the motorway. They understand that the planet needs localist autonomy, with its decentralized national decisions, and also external openness with gradually stronger cooperative international governance. The former should constrain nascent international governance from choosing prematurely ambitious goals. The latter is required to constrain individual nations from drifting too badly astray. An Okun-inspired paraphrase is pertinent: Local autonomy and external openness each need a place, and each needs to be kept in its place.

Pragmatic incrementalism seeks substantial forward progress over time. But it accepts the likelihood that progress has to be gradual and cumulative. It does not urge intergovernmental cooperation and international institutions to perform unrealistic miracles. The first half of its motto is, "Do not unrealistically ask for too much, too soon." But progress has been badly lagging behind the rapid pace at which collective-governance problems with cross-border dimensions have been evolving. Many needed decisions have been fainthearted or deferred altogether. They should be more expeditious, even ambitious. The complete motto of pragmatic incrementalism is, "Do not unrealistically ask for too much, too soon. But for goodness' sake, do not be too timid either!"

Cooperative compromise governance for our fractious planet will continue to be messy and accident-prone. New governance uncertainties will emerge. The task for policymakers—finding appropriate compromise combinations of national and international policies—will never be completed. Turbulence may be necessary to galvanize progress, but it would be preferable if increments could accumulate without the spur of turbulence.

Art Okun was prescient: "At the moment we are experiencing a disturbing divisiveness of attitudes. . . . Instead of blending the values of capitalism and democracy, many are pitting them against each other. Instead of compromising, we are polarizing. The nation sorely needs a serious dialogue and a major educational undertaking to develop the enlightened attitudes of compromise."[3]

Progress, albeit slow and halting, is definitely possible. History is, again, replete with positive achievements resulting from international cooperation.

Without progress, the major worry persists: Will our higgledy-piggledy planet spawn failed higgledy-piggledy governance?

With sufficient progress, collective governance can generate order that helps to offset the disorder that might otherwise prevail.

It is not too much to hope that the planet's nations can function better by nurturing international comity. Perhaps decisions could even move forward briskly rather than on tiptoe? And, ideally, governance authorities can learn how to forge better collaborative international agreements and how to more successfully allocate governance responsibilities to international and national institutions.

---

3. Okun (2015, p. 148).

# Postscript: Emergence of
## the Coronavirus Pandemic

The writing of this book was completed in November 2019. At that time, only epidemiology scientists envisaged—certainly I did not imagine—a coronavirus pandemic capable of ravaging health and economic livelihoods throughout the world.

The COVID-19 infection emerged in Wuhan, China, in December 2019. During the next three months, it spread rapidly across national borders to the rest of Asia, the United States, and Europe. By April 2020 the pandemic was a worldwide crisis.

As the infectious outbreaks proliferated, national as well as local governing authorities acted haltingly and with little coordination. Few jurisdictions adopted systematic measures to diagnose and constrain the pandemic. Testing for the virus, aggregated collection and processing of testing data, and accessible sharing of those data were inadequate. Lockdown restrictions and social-distancing mitigation were at first confusingly implemented. Surveillance and monitoring of infected individuals was poor. Initial planning for intensive care for severe cases and for provision of needed medical equipment was often inept. Public supports for crash efforts to develop vaccines and new treatment strategies were uncoordinated.

Communications across borders were likewise halting and

ineffectual. The inevitable centripetal leanings toward national localism (see chapter 3) were intensified. Competitive closings of borders to protect local residents were initiated with little regard for outside foreigners. Individual national authorities competed, frequently without consulting and collaborating with others, to obtain needed medical equipment. Pharmaceutical companies racing to create vaccines seemed as concerned about national pecking orders and prospective distribution controls as much as they were about collective scientific progress. The World Health Organization became a center of dispute rather than a primary institutional focus for international cooperation.

The COVID-19 pandemic is quintessentially a global crisis. In the initial months, sadly, the worst failures of adequate communications and collective measures were on the international front. Cross-border consultations and global cooperation were urgently needed. For the most part they did not occur. Insufficient attention, for example, was paid to limiting cross-border transmission of the virus in mutually beneficial ways. Planning and execution of control measures were, yes, higgledy-piggledy rather than systematic. Central banks of the major nations, consulting together, initially adopted bold and helpful actions; those were exceptions to otherwise deficient cooperation. Another exception was the prompt international consultations and cooperation among research scientists. But only limited international coordination existed for public-good efforts among governing authorities and the World Health Organization to create new vaccines and medical treatments. Successful use of new vaccines, once produced, depends on wise distribution. Initially, demand for vaccines globally will far outstrip what manufacturers can supply. Agreements among nations, negotiated beforehand, would be very helpful to ensure that vaccines are allocated by priority needs and locations. Without such agreements, inadequate early supplies could be entangled in bidding wars, hoarding, and ineffective vaccination campaigns. More generally, governing authorities should increase future support for collaborative scientific advances in medical knowledge about viruses.

Shortcomings of international cooperation about the pandemic seemed evident even in the early consultatiohs conducted through the World Health Organization. Then miscommunications and tensions about the origins of the pandemic and the effectiveness of the World Health Organization itself emerged among its dominant member nations, China and the United States.

Pandemic issues are inseparable from issues of national security, economic policy, and diplomacy. For other major nations—European, Asian, or emerging-market, not only the United States—China is a systemic rival and an economic competitor in the pursuit of technological leadership. China's record on democratic freedoms and human rights is badly blemished. Governance arrangements for Hong Kong and Taiwan pose fractious controversies. Nonetheless, China is also a negotiating partner with whom a balance of interests must be worked out and a cooperation partner with whom some basic objectives are aligned. Multinational institutions such as the World Health Organization can be jointly beneficial for fostering the negotiations and cooperation. The governance records of all nations have blemishes and could benefit from improvements. The separate fractious interests of China, the United States, and all other nations, great and small, can be mutually served by working together through commonly supported forums that catalyze needed consultations about shared challenges. That underlying goal is the fundamental rationale for international institutions such as the World Health Organization, the International Monetary Fund, the World Bank, and the World Trade Organization.

Abominable failures of global leadership by the United States took place from 2017 to 2020 (chapter 7). Comparably harmful failures in U.S. leadership occurred in the early months of the global pandemic. There was little positive reaching out by U.S.

governing authorities. Examples of "America First" national localism and backsliding from international cooperation were dominant. Public threats that the United States would withdraw from the World Health Organization are particularly despicable. Such threats are inimical for the long-run interests of the United States itself and collectively damaging for the future interests of all nations.

———————

The coronavirus crisis exemplifies the themes of this book. Inadequate diagnoses and control measures persist. Failures of leadership continue in many national and local jurisdictions. Successful development and dissemination of vaccines and achievement of high levels of herd immunity appear to be, at best, months into the future.

With no clear resolutions in sight of the health, economic, and political miseries of the pandemic, the spring of 2020 is too early a time to attempt a balanced analytical perspective. The wide range of uncertainties could be resolved in numerous different ways. Some are relatively benign. But others could be catastrophic. The worst imaginable future outcomes for the planet would include enhanced aggressive hostility between China and the United States. And with as yet little evidence of focused cross-border and international-institution efforts to improve mutually beneficial governance, one cannot yet assess the consequences of the pandemic for international cooperation over the longer run.

This book thus ventures into an uncertain turbulent world without an assessment of the global pandemic. It comes with a reiterated prayer that future improvements in cross-border collective comity and governance will generate more cooperative order to help offset the higgledy-piggledy disorder and tensions that may otherwise prevail.

# References

Abbott, Kenneth W., and Duncan Snidal, "Hard and Soft Law in International Governance," in *Legalization and World Politics*, a special issue of *International Organization* 54 (Summer 2000), pp. 421–456.

Abbott, Kenneth W., and Duncan Snidal, "Law, Legalization and Politics: An Agenda for the Next Generation of IR-IL Scholars," in *Interdisciplinary Perspectives on International Law and International Relations: The State of the Art*, edited by Jeffrey L. Dunoff and Mark A. Pollock (Cambridge University Press, 2013).

Abbott, Kenneth W., and Duncan Snidal, "Why States Act Through Formal Organizations," *Journal of Conflict Resolution* 42 (1998), pp. 3–32.

Ahearne, Alan, and others, "Global Governance: An Agenda for Europe," Bruegel Policy Brief Series, Issue 2006/07 (Brussels: Bruegel, December 2006).

Akerlof, George A., and Rachel E. Kranton, *Identity Economics: How Our Identities Shape Our Work, Wages, and Well-Being* (Princeton University Press, 2011).

Akerlof, George A., and Robert J. Shiller, *Phishing for Phools: The Economics of Manipulation and Deception* (Princeton University Press, 2015).

Appiah, Kwame Anthony, *Cosmopolitanism: Ethics in a World of Strangers* (New York: Norton, 2006).

Austin, Benjamin, Edward Glaeser, and Lawrence Summers, "Saving the Heartland: Place-Based Policies in 21st Century America," *Brookings Papers on Economic Activity* (Brookings Institution, Spring 2018).

Baldwin, Richard E., *The Great Convergence: Information Technology and the New Globalization* (Belknap Press of Harvard University Press, 2016).

Baldwin, Richard E., "The World Trade Organization and the Future of Multilateralism," *Journal of Economic Perspectives*, vol. 30, no.1 (Winter 2016, pp. 95–116).

Bank of England, Financial Policy Committee and Prudential Regulation Committee, *Discussion Paper: The 2021 Biennial Exploratory Scenario on the Financial Risks from Climate Change* (December 2019).

Barrett, Scott, *Environment & Statecraft: The Strategy of Environmental Treaty-Making* (Oxford University Press, 2003).

Barrett, Scott, "Self-Enforcing International Environmental Agreements," *Oxford Economic Papers* 46 (1994, pp. 878–894).

Berkman, Paul Arthur, and others, eds., *Science Diplomacy: Antarctica, Science, and the Governance of International Spaces,* from the Smithsonian Contributions to Knowledge series (Smithsonian Institution Scholarly Press, 2011).

Berlin, Isaiah, *Liberty* (collected essays), edited by Henry Hardy (Oxford University Press, 2002).

Bernanke, Ben S., *The Courage to Act: A Memoir of a Crisis and Its Aftermath* (New York: W. W. Norton, 2015).

Bernanke, Ben S., and others, eds., *First Responders: Inside the U.S. Strategy for Fighting the 2007–2009 Global Financial Crisis* (Yale University Press, 2020).

Bertaut, Carol C., Beau Bressler, and Stephanie E. Curcuru, "Globalization and the Geography of Capital Flows," Federal Reserve Board, FED Notes no. 20190906 (https://ssrn.com/abstract=3473083 or http://dx.doi.org/10.17016/23807172.2446).

Bowles, Samuel, *The Moral Economy: Why Good Incentives Are No Substitute for Good Citizens* (Yale University Press, 2016).

Bowles, Samuel, and Herbert Gintis, *A Cooperative Species: Human Reciprocity and Its Evolution* (Princeton University Press, 2011).

Brown, Patrick T., "The Dark Side of Social Capital." *National Affairs*, no. 40 (Summer 2019, pp. 107–116).

Bryant, Ralph C., *Crisis Prevention and Prosperity Management for the World Economy. Pragmatic Choices for International Financial Governance* (Brookings Institution, 2004).

Bryant, Ralph C., *International Coordination of National Stabilization Policies*, Integrating National Economies series (Brookings Institution, 1995).

Bryant, Ralph C., *International Financial Intermediation* (Brookings Institution, 1987).

Bryant, Ralph C., *Money and Monetary Policy in Interdependent Nations* (Brookings Institution, 1980).

Bryant, Ralph C., *Turbulent Waters: Cross-Border Finance and International Governance* (Brookings Institution, 2003).

Bryant, Ralph C., Dale W. Henderson, and Torbjorn Becker, *Maintaining Financial Stability in an Open Economy: Sweden in the Global Crisis and Beyond* (Stockholm Sweden: SNS Forlag, 2012).

Collier, Paul, *Exodus: Immigration and Multiculturalism in the 21st Century* (London: Penguin Books, 2014).

Cooper, Richard N., *Economic Policy in an Interdependent World* (MIT Press, 1986).

Cooper, Richard N., "Worldwide or Regional Integration: Is There an Optimal Size of the Integrated Area?" Originally published in 1974 and reprinted in *Economic Policy an Interdependent World* (MIT Press, 1986, pp. 123–136).

Cumberland, John H., James R. Hibbs, and Irving Hoch, eds. 1982. *The Economics of Managing Chlorofluorocarbons: Stratospheric Ozone and Climate Issues* (Washington, D.C.: Resources for the Future, Inc., 1982).

de Tocqueville, Alexis, *Democracy in America*, edited by Phillips Bradley (New York: Vintage Books, 1945).

Dervis, Kemal, and Sebastian Strauss, "The Real Obstacle to Climate Action," op-ed, Brookings Institution (August 20, 2019).

Edge, Rochelle M., and J. Nellie Liang, "New Financial Stability Governance Structures and Central Banks," Hutchins Center Working Paper #50, Brookings Institution (February 2019).

Egel, Naomi, "Order and Disorder in Today's Global Order" (report), Princeton Workshop on Global Governance, Council on Foreign Relations, International Institutions and Global Governance program (June 4–5, 2015).

Egginton, William, *The Splintering of the American Mind. Identity Politics, Inequality, and Community on Today's College Campuses* (London: Bloomsbury, 2018).

Fisher, Max, and Amanda Taub, "Trump Wants to Make It Hard to Get Asylum. Other Countries Feel the Same," *New York Times* (November 2–3, 2018).

Føllesdal, Andreas, "Federalism," *Stanford Encyclopedia of Philosophy*, edited by Edward N. Zalta (Spring 2014).

Friedman, Thomas, *The Lexus and the Olive Tree* (New York: Farrar, Straus & Giroux, 1999).

Gessen, Masha, "Trump's Opponents Aren't Arguing for 'Open Borders' —But Maybe They Should," *The New Yorker* (June 22, 2018).

Goodhart, David, *The Road to Somewhere: The Populist Revolt and the Future of Politics* (London: C. Hurst & Co., 2017).

Hanson, Gordon, and Craig McIntosh, "Is the Mediterranean the New Rio Grande? U.S. and EU Immigration Pressures in the Long Run," *Journal of Economic Perspectives* 30 (Fall 2016, pp. 58–82).

Hayek, Friedrich A., *The Road to Serfdom* (University of Chicago Press, 1944).

Helliwell, John F., ed., *The Contribution of Human and Social Capital to Sustained Economic Growth and Well-Being* (Ottawa: Human Resources Development, Canada, 2000).

Helliwell, John F., *How Much Do National Borders Matter?* (Brookings Institution, 1998).

Helliwell, John F., Richard Layard, and Jeffrey D. Sachs, *World Happiness Report 2018* (New York: Sustainable Development Solutions Network, 2018).

Helliwell, John F., and others, "Good Governance and National Well-being: What Are the Linkages?" *OECD Working Papers on Public Governance,* no. 25.

Hendrickson, Clara, Mark Muro, and William A. Galston, "Countering the Geography of Discontent: Strategies for Left-Behind Places" report, Brookings Institution (November 2018).

Hirsch, Fred, *Social Limits to Growth* (Harvard University Press, 1976).

Hirschman, Albert O., *Exit, Voice, and Loyalty: Responses to Decline in Firms, Organizations, and States* (Harvard University Press, 1970).

Horn, Henrik, and Andre Sapir, "Border Carbon Tariffs: Giving Up on Trade to Save the Climate?" August 29, 2019 (www.bruegel .org/2019/08/border-carbon-tariffs-giving-up-on-trade-to -save-the-climate/).

Intergovernmental Panel on Climate Change (IPCC), *2019 Refinement to the 2006 IPCC Guidelines for National Greenhouse Gas Inventories*, United Nations (May 2019).

Intergovernmental Panel on Climate Change (IPCC), "Climate Change and Land," IPCC Special Report, United Nations (August 2019).

Intergovernmental Panel on Climate Change (IPCC), "Special Report on the Ocean and Cryosphere in a Changing Climate," United Nations (September 2019).

Intergovernmental Panel on Climate Change (IPCC), "Special Report on Climate Change, Desertification, Land Degradation, Sustainable Land Management, Food Security, and Greenhouse Gas Fluxes in Terrestrial Ecosystems," United Nations (August 2019).

International Monetary Fund, World Bank, and World Trade Organization, "Making Trade the Engine of Growth for All: The Case for Trade and for Policies to Facilitate Adjustment," report prepared for discussion at the Meeting of G-20 Sherpas, Frankfurt (www.imf.org/~/media/Files/Publications/PP/041017joint-wto-wb-imf-trade-paper.ashx).

Kahler, Miles, and David A. Lake, eds., *Governance in a Global Economy: Political Authority in Transition* (Princeton University Press, 2003).

Kamarck, Elaine, "The Challenging Politics of Climate Change," Brookings Institution (September 23, 2019).

Keohane, Robert O., *After Hegemony: Cooperation and Discord in the World Political Economy* (Princeton University Press, 1984).

Keohane, Robert O., and Joseph S. Nye Jr., *Power and Interdependence: World Politics in Transition*, Third Edition (New York: Longman, 2000).

Kipling, Rudyard, *Debits and Credits* (London: Macmillan, 1926).

Kohn, Donald L., "Macroprudential Policy: Implementation and Effectiveness," speech given at the European Central Bank, Frankfurt (April 27, 2016).

Koremenos, Barbara, *The Continent of International Law: Explaining Agreement Design* (Cambridge University Press, 2016).

Koremenos, Barbara, Charles Lipson, and Duncan Snidal, "The Rational Design of International Institutions," *International Organization* vol. 55, no. 4 (August 2001, pp. 761–800).

Krugman, Paul, "Trump Makes America Irresponsible Again: Why 'Tariff' Isn't a 'Beautiful' Word," *New York Times* (June 3, 2019).

Lane, Philip R., and Gian Maria Milesi-Ferretti, "Cross-Border Investment in Small International Financial Centers," *International Finance* vol. 14, no. 2 (2011, pp. 301–330).

Lane, Philip R., and Gian Maria Milesi-Ferretti, "The External Wealth of Nations Mark II Database," originally published in *Journal of International Economics* vol. 73 (November 2007, 223–250) and updated and extended in 2011.

Lane, Philip R., and Gian Maria Milesi-Ferretti, "The External Wealth of Nations Mark II: Revised and Extended Estimates of External Assets and Liabilities," *Journal of International Economics* vol. 73 (2007, pp. 223–250).

Lane, Philip R., and Gian Maria Milesi-Ferretti, "The External Wealth of Nations Revisited: International Financial Integration in the Aftermath of the Global Financial Crisis," International Monetary Fund (February 2018).

Leonhardt, David, "Economists Have Workable Policy Ideas for Addressing Climate Change. But What If They're Politically Impossible?" *New York Times Magazine* (April 9, 2019).

Liang, J. Nellie, "Rethinking Financial Stability and Macroprudential Policy," Brookings Institution (December 4, 2017).

Liang, J. Nellie, "Eight Lessons for Fighting the Next Financial Crisis," Brookings Institution (September 13, 2018).

Liu, Weifeng, and others, "Global Economic and Environmental Outcomes of the Paris Agreement," Global and Energy Economics Discussion Paper, Brookings Institution (January 7, 2019).

Lomborg, Bjørn, "The Dangers of Climate Doomsayers," *Project Syndicate* (August 19, 2019).

Lowe, Sam, "Should the EU Tax Imported $CO_2$?" *Insight*, Centre for European Reform (September 24, 2019).

Maier, Charles S., *Leviathan 2.0: Inventing Modern Statehood* (Belknap Press of Harvard University Press, 2012).

Maier, Charles S., *Once Within Borders: Territories of Power, Wealth, and Belonging Since 1500* (Harvard University Press, 2016).

McKibbin, Warwick J., "Australia Can't Run Away from a Carbon Price Any Longer," op-ed published in *Australian Financial Review* (December 4, 2018).

McKibbin, Warwick J., and Peter J. Wilcoxen, "A Credible Foundation for Long Term International Cooperation on Climate Change," Working Paper draft (April 2006). Revised in *Architecture for Agreement: Addressing Global Climate Change in the Post-Kyoto World*, edited by Joseph Aldy and Robert Stavins (Cambridge University Press, 2007).

McKibbin, Warwick J., and Peter J. Wilcoxen, "Building on Kyoto: Towards a Realistic Global Climate Agreement," Policy Brief 08-01, Brookings Energy Security Initiative, Brookings Institution (November 2008).

Meek, James, "Brexit and Myths of Englishness," *London Review of Books*, vol. 40, no. 19 (October 11, 2018).

Metcalf, Gilbert E., "On the Economics of a Carbon Tax for the United States," *Brookings Papers on Economic Activity* (Brookings Institution, Spring 2019).

Mill, John Stuart, *Considerations on Representative Government* (1861) (New York: Liberal Arts Press, 1958).

Mill, John Stuart, *On Liberty* (1859) (London: Longmans, Green, Reader, Dyer; 1869).

Nordhaus, William D., "Climate Change: The Ultimate Challenge for Economics," Nobel Prize lecture December 2018, published in *American Economic Review*, vol. 109, no. 6 (June 2019, pp. 1091–2014).

Obstfeld, Maurice, "Trilemmas and Trade-offs: Living with Financial Globalisation," BIS Working Paper No. 480, with comments by Otmar Issing and Takatoshi Ito (Basel, Switzerland: Bank for International Settlements, Monetary and Economic Department, January 2015).

Obstfeld, Maurice, and Alan M. Taylor, "International Monetary Relations: Taking Finance Seriously," *Journal of Economic Perspectives*, vol. 31, no. 3 (Summer 2017, pp. 3–28).

Obstfeld, Maurice, Jay C. Shambaugh, and Alan M. Taylor, "Monetary Sovereignty, Exchange Rates, and Capital Controls: The Trilemma in the Interwar Period," CIDER Working Paper C04-134m, Center for International and Development Economics Research (University of California-Berkeley, May 2004).

Obstfeld, Maurice, Jay C. Shambaugh, and Alan M. Taylor, "The Trilemma in History: Trade-offs among Exchange Rates, Monetary Policies, and Capital Mobility," CIDER Working Paper C04-133, Center for International and Development Economics Research (University of California-Berkeley, May 2004).

Okun, Arthur M., *Equality and Efficiency: The Big Tradeoff* (Brookings Institution, 1975, 2015).

Olson, Mancur, *The Logic of Collective Action: Public Goods and the Theory of Groups*, Second Edition (Harvard University Press, 1971).

Ostrom, Elinor, "Collective Action and the Evolution of Social Norms," *Journal of Economic Perspectives* vol. 14 (Summer 2000, pp. 137–158).

Ostrom, Elinor, *Governing the Commons: The Evolution of Institutions for Collective Action* (Cambridge University Press, 1990, reprinted 1994).

Patrick, Stewart, *The Sovereignty Wars: Reconciling America with the World* (Brookings Institution, 2017).

Patrick, Stewart, "The Unruled World: The Case for 'Good Enough' Global Governance," *Foreign Affairs* (January–February 2014).

Putnam, Robert D., *Bowling Alone: The Collapse and Revival of American Community* (New York: Simon and Schuster, 2000).

Putnam, Robert D., "Social Capital: Measurement and Consequences," in *The Contribution of Human and Social Capital to Sustained Economic Growth and Well-Being*, edited by John F. Helliwell (Ottawa, Canada: Human Resources Development, 2000).

Raustiala, Kal, "The Architecture of International Cooperation: Transgovernmental Networks and the Future of International Law," *Virginia Journal of International Law* vol. 43, no. 1 (2002).

Rey, Hélène, "Dilemma Not Trilemma: The Global Financial Cycle and Monetary Policy Independence," presentation at Federal Reserve Bank of Kansas City Symposium, *Global Dimensions of Unconventional Monetary Policy*, Jackson Hole, Wyoming (September 2013).

Rodrik, Dani, *The Globalization Paradox: Democracy and the Future of the World Economy* (New York: W. W. Norton & Company, 2011).

Rodrik, Dani, "Governance of Economic Globalization," in *Governance in a Globalizing World*, edited by Joseph S. Nye and John D. Donahue (Brookings Institution, 2000).

Rodrik, Dani, "More on the Political Trilemmas of the Global Economy," March 11, 2016 (https://rodrik.typepad.com/dani_rodriks_weblog/2016/03/more-on-the-political-trilemma-of-the-global-economy.html).

Schoenmaker, Dirk, *Governance of International Banking: The Financial Trilemma* (Oxford University Press, 2013).

Shambaugh, Jay, and Ryan Nunn, eds., "Place-Based Policies for Shared Economic Growth," *The Hamilton Project*, Brookings Institution (September 2018).

Slaughter, Anne-Marie, *A New World Order* (Princeton University Press, 2004).

Talbott, Strobe, *The Great Experiment: The Story of Ancient Empires, Modern States, and the Quest for a Global Nation* (New York: Simon & Schuster, 2008).

Talbott, Strobe, "Monnet's Brandy & Europe's Fate," *Brookings Essays*, Brookings Institution (February 11, 2014) (http://csweb.brookings.edu/content/research/essays/2014/monnets-brandy-and-europes-fate.html).

Traub, James, "The Hard Truth about Refugees," op-ed, *New York Times* (March 7, 2017).

UNHCR, *Convention and Protocol Relating to the Status of Refugees* (Geneva: December 2010).

VanGrasstek, Craig, *The History and Future of the World Trade Organization* (Geneva: World Trade Organization, 2013).

Wallace-Wells, David. *The Uninhabitable Earth: A Story of the Future* (New York: Penguin Books, 2019).

Weisman, Steven R., *The Great Tradeoff: Confronting Moral Conflicts in the Era of Globalization* (Washington, D.C.: Peterson Institute for International Economics, 2016).

Young, Oran R., *International Cooperation: Building Regimes for Natural Resources and the Environment* (Cornell University Press, 1989).

# Index

169